MARCO ⊕ POLO

Tips

COSTA BRAVA

BARCELONA

FRANCE
CH
ITALY
Bilbao
ANDORRA
Costa
Brava
Madrid
SPAIN
Corsica
(F)
Barcelona
Valencia
Balearic
Sardinia
Islands (E)
(I)
*Mediterranean
Sea*
ALGERIA

www.marco-polo.com

The best Insider Tips → p. 4

INSIDER TIP

Best of ... → p. 6

Alt Empordà → p. 32

Baix Empordà → p. 50

SYMBOLS

INSIDER TIP	Insider Tip
★	Highlight
●●●●	Best of ...
☼	Scenic view
☺	Responsible travel: fair trade principles and the environment respected

**PRICE CATEGORIES
HOTELS**

Expensive   over 100 euros

Moderate   70–100 euros

Budget   under 70 euros

Prices are for a double room, usually with breakfast

**PRICE CATEGORIES
RESTAURANTS**

Expensive   over 30 euros

Moderate   20–30 euros

Budget   under 20 euros

Prices are for a three-course meal including water or wine

On the cover: The most easterly point in Spain: Cap de Creus p. 37 | On the trail of Salvador Dalí p. 38

CONTENTS

Girona and La Selva → p. 70

Barcelona → p. 82

Trips & Tours → p. 88

Road atlas → p. 118

DID YOU KNOW?

Timeline → p. 12
Local specialities → p. 26
Books & Films → p. 68
Budgeting → p. 108
Currency converter → p. 109
Weather in Barcelona → p. 111

MAPS IN THE GUIDEBOOK

(120 A1) Page numbers and coordinates refer to the road atlas
(O) Site/address located off the map. Coordinates are also given for places that are not marked on the road atlas
(U A1) Coordinates refer to the street map of Barcelona inside the back cover
Girona, Figueres → p. 126
Tossa, Sant Feliu → p. 127

**INSIDE BACK COVER:
PULL-OUT MAP →**

PULL-OUT MAP

(∭ A–B 2–3) Refers to the removable pull-out map
(∭ a–b 2–3) Refers to the additional inset map on the pull-out map

The best MARCO POLO Insider Tips

Our top 15 Insider Tips

INSIDER TIP Beneath fragrant wisteria ...

... is where you can enjoy a meal in the Rostei restaurant in Begur, if you manage to get one of the 20 places outside. Inside there is a cosy atmosphere under in a vaulted ceiling → **p. 52**

INSIDER TIP Welcome the arrival of summer

The Sant Joan Festival on 24 June is accompanied by lots of noise on the streets, fireworks and a great atmosphere – for free (photo above) → **p. 103**

INSIDER TIP Taking it easy

In the Casino de Cadaqués, the town's meeting place, life gets started at 5 o'clock in the morning with a little tipple: a coffee and brandy is the breakfast of choice for locals → **p. 36**

INSIDER TIP Charming fishing village

You will not find any massive hotels in El Port de la Selva, but instead a well cared for town with a large port and quiet bathing bays, also popular with locals → **p. 44**

INSIDER TIP A bird's eye view

A circular walk high above the coast provides fantastic views of the sea and the bathing bays lying far below, against the backdrop of the medieval town of Begur → **p. 53**

INSIDER TIP Market day

In the medieval surroundings of La Bisbal's Friday market you can buy not only fruit and vegetables, but also clothes and household goods → **p. 55**

INSIDER TIP Village peace and quiet

In addition to beautifully restored buildings, Cruïlles offers an authentic village lifestyle, a church, a monastery and 11th century castle ruins. Surrounded by lovely, quiet countryside → **p. 56**

INSIDER TIP Eating like the fishermen

The fishermen like their *suquet*, fish stew with beans and potatoes, thick and hearty → **p. 25**

INSIDER TIP Boat processions and dancing

The patron saint of fishermen is celebrated each year on 16 July. After a boat procession at sea, the fun continues back on shore with dancing, picnics and plenty of wine → p. 103

INSIDER TIP Fish large and small

Visitors can learn everything there is to know about fishing in the Museu de la Pesca in Palamós: local fish species, the history and development of fishing methods, the life of fishermen yesterday and today, and lots more → p. 57

INSIDER TIP Elegant picnic at the vineyard

With ham, cold meats, cheese and, of course, the Terra Remota house wine, your every wish is fulfilled. Beforehand you can enjoy an interesting tour the modern winery some 13km/8mi south of Figueres → p. 41

INSIDER TIP It does not get any fresher

The catch of the day is sold in Palamós auction hall, which immediately whets the appetite for a delicious fish meal → p. 57

INSIDER TIP Sleep like royalty

In the atmospheric tower room at the luxury hotel Castell d'Empordà in Bisbal, guests sleep surrounded by historic furnishings and the relaxing stillness of the wonderfully rural countryside → p. 55

INSIDER TIP Crystal clear water

A swim in the bay at Aiguablava is a real experience; especially early in the morning when the beach is still relatively empty (photo below) → p. 54

INSIDER TIP High up on the cliffs...

... there is one of the quaintest bars on the Costa Brava: the Cap de Creus bar in Cadaqués. This is where to escape from the occasionally stormy winds on the coast → p. 34

BEST OF ...

GREAT PLACES FOR FREE
Discover new places and save money

FOR FREE

● *More about the sea*
You can learn everything there is about the Mediterranean, and lots more, from the collections of the unique *Can Quintana* museum in Toroella de Montgrí, and admission's free → p. 66

● *Services in splendid churches*
Church-going tourists may attend services in all the churches on the Costa Brava, and can at the same time have a good look at some splendid buildings without paying a penny. One example is the *cathedral* in *Girona* on Sundays (10am–2pm) a visit to which is otherwise subject to an admission charge → p. 74

● *Free ride*
There is a toll, a *peaje,* on Spanish motorways. But there is no charge for driving on the *autovia* – a road running parallel to the motorway. For example, the NII parallel to the AP-7 between Giron and Caldes de Malavella, is just as good a road → p. 76

● *Walk to the dolls*
There are *guided summer walks* in Castell d'Aro through the historic town centre followed by a visit to the local *Museu de la Niña*, the doll museum, exhibiting dolls from many countries – and all of it is for free → p. 63

● *Heading south ...*
... thousands of migratory birds stop over in the *L'Empordà* wetlands, where a large nature park has been established. There are hides from which amateur ornithologists can enjoy a close up view of storks, ducks, geese and other bird species, as close as would normally only be possible in a zoo → p. 49

● *Go to a concert*
In the venerable *London Bar* in Barcelona you can still enjoy free concerts performed by various music groups. Admission may be free, but the same can't be said for the beer (photo) → p. 87

●●●● Dots in guidebook refer to 'Best of ...' tips

ONLY ON THE COSTA BRAVA
Unique experiences

● *Sun, sea and sand*
Statistically there are only 55 days of rain a year on
the Costa Brava. Guaranteed sunshine and more
than a dozen *beaches* – such as the one in *Platja
d'Aro*, awarded the Blue Flag for cleanliness –
make the Costa Brava a first class coast for
swimming and sunbathing → p. 62

● *We're amongst giants*
They are at almost every village festival: the
gegants – giant figures made of papier mâché – which stride in pairs through the crowds
to the utter delight of children (photo) → p. 20

● *National dance*
The *sardana* was banned during the Franco era, but
today people are dancing it again – spontaneously, at
festivals and at the annual competition in Sant Feliu de Guíxols
→ p. 23, 103

● *Beyond the beach: the Middle Ages*
Catalonia is a land of contrasts: new and old, quiet and noisy. A few
miles inland you will come across places where time seems to have
stood still. Narrow streets, stone buildings, carved portals and idyllic
squares. One example is *Pals* → p. 54

● *Cultured tourism*
Cultured tourism with lots of charm and without high-rise buildings –
that's also part of the Costa Brava, and *Cadaqués* is a good example:
former fishing port, Picasso's holiday resort, Dalí's summer residence
and later an international hippy commune → p. 32, 38

● *Calas: bays*
The bays – *calas* – which make Costa Brava the 'wild coast', are often
remote, hidden away between rocks and surrounded by fragrant pine
woods. You will find crystal clear, refreshing water at places such as
Llançà and *Sant Feliu de Guíxols* → p. 44, 65

● *Entertainment centre*
The picture people have of cheap holidays on the Costa Brava is based on
Lloret de Mar. For some, mostly the younger generation, the former fish-
ing village is an entertainment paradise with endless discos and parties.
While others find all that is needed for a successful family holiday → p. 76

ONLY IN

BEST OF ...

● *Keep dry with a stroll round the market*
Barcelona in the rain? Visit the large *Boqueria* market hall where you can buy – and consume – various delicacies. And you can have a browse in the charming shops in the surrounding streets → p. 84

● *Creative pottery*
You can watch clay being transformed into pottery in the *Terracotta Museu* in Bisbal. As soon as the sun comes out again, you can have a close look at the creative finished products in the shops on the main street (photo) → p. 54

● *Get thee to a nunnery!*
The *Benedictine monastery*, with an 11th century church and the tomb of St Daniel – who gave the monastery its name – has a beautiful two-storey Romanesque cloister that offers room for some silent reflection → p. 76

● *Change trains ...*
... was what passengers had to do in Portbou on the border between Spain and France because the trains ran on different gauges. Though today this procedure is a distant memory, the *railway station* built by Eiffel with its massive iron construction is still worth a visit → p. 45

● *Sharks and small fish*
Immerse yourself in the underwater world of the sea. The Oceanarium in the *Aquarium* in Barcelona is particularly spectacular. A huge pool with numerous species you can observe from an underwater tunnel. The top stars: the tiger sharks → p. 101

● *For the bottle*
Cork is being increasingly replaced as a bottle seal by synthetic seals or screw tops. But the natural product is the star of the show in the *Museu del Suro* in Palafrugell → p. 61

RAIN

RELAX AND CHILL OUT
Take it easy and spoil yourself

● *Warm water relaxation*

As long ago as in Roman times, people would come to the *Caldes de Malavella* thermal baths in search of rest and relaxation. Since 1840 guests at the spa resorts *Balneari Prats* and *Vichy Catalán* have been revitalised with various treatments → **p. 76**

● *Ship ahoy*

In Palamos you can spend the day at sea on board the sailing yacht *Rafael*: coves, swimming, sun and a sea breeze all ensure a restful experience → **p. 58**

● *A stroll in the park*

The gardens at *Santa Clotilde* are one of the most beautiful parks on the Costa Brava. Small squares invite to you sit and relax. With peace and quiet, observation points with sea views, pretty fountains and typical Mediterranean trees, you will quickly forget all the hubbub of nearby Lloret de Mar (photo) → **p. 79**

● *Delights of chocolate*

The *Granja La Pallaresa* is one of the delights in Barcelona's old town alleys where you can indulge your sweet tooth. In this traditional café, much frequented by locals, the elderly ladies like to order a *suizo* (a Swiss) thick hot chocolate topped with cream → **p. 86**

● *A refreshing plunge*

Aiguafreda is a beautiful small bay in Begur with crystal clear water and surrounded by fragrant pines – an ideal place to switch off. You can enjoy a cool drink in the nearby restaurant → **p. 53**

● *Time out in a castle and wine cellar*

The magnificent atmosphere of the 14th century *Castell de Peralada* is enough to transport visitors into another world. After visiting the museum you can taste a fine wine or two in the historic wine cellar → **p. 40**

INTRODUCTION

DISCOVER THE COSTA BRAVA!

The stretch of Costa Brava (wild coast) is more than 200km/125mi in length, running from the Pyrenees, which rise up like a defensive wall between France and Spain, to the town of Blanes. The journalist Ferran Agulló is said to have coined the term in September 1908 in an article published in the Catalan newspaper *La Veu de Catalunya*, referring to the rugged landscape of this piece of Mediterranean coast. He must, of course, have had the landscape in mind and hardly the wild nights in the tourist centres, because these didn't exist in his day. But the fact remains that the north of the autonomous region of Catalonia borders the Mediterranean with a really wild and rugged coast.

Costa Brava: this means small fishing villages in the north, such as Cadaqués and Palamós; charming seaside resorts such as Sant Feliu and Tossa and cultural centres such as Girona and Figueres. If want to enjoy more than just beach life, there are lots of ways to have an active holiday. In the Cap de Creus and Empordà nature parks

Photo: The bay at Sa Riera

Pals: a picturesque medieval old town set in lush countryside

there are some magnificent hikes while the coast offers diving, sailing and surfing. And there are small Spanish Catalan towns in the hinterland waiting to be explored.

A land of sea and mountains – and in between there is not much more than 50km/30mi. In addition to some major plains, such as the river marshes east of Figueres or at La Bisbal, the countryside has mainly gently rolling hills. Once these were covered by extensive pine and oak forests, much of which was destroyed by excessive ship building in the Middle Ages. However, bays bordered by pine trees are still characteristic of this part of the Mediterranean coast.

Fishing, cork oaks and agriculture

The prawns from Palamós and the sardines from the north coast have made the Costa Brava popular in Spain but it is not only famous for fishing catches. Inland from the coast there is a flourishing and varied agriculture. The villages are well cared for, the

2nd century BC
Roman legions occupy the coast of Catalonia and shape the country's culture for more than 200 years

712
The Moors advance on the Iberian Peninsula

Around 800
Charlemagne liberates parts of Catalonia from the Moors

9th century
Formation of counties under Barcelona's leadership

Around 1740
Greater economic strength with the rise of a textile industry, Barcelona becomes the economic capital

1888
World Exhibition in

fields well tilled. Here you can see olive groves, vineyards and cornfields, fields full of artichokes, tomatoes and aubergines, as well as oak and cork oak woods. The cork oaks formed the basis of a significant industry for centuries but, given the competition from synthetic products, natural cork has today lost much of its importance. The further inland you go, the more rugged it gets. Soon the summits of the Pyrenees and their foothills loom up, and instead of tractors it is flocks of sheep which cross your path.

The fertile land provides the material for pottery

The land is rich in water. Some streams and rivers come down from the mountains and flow into the sea. The two most important are the Riu Ter and the Riu Fluvià. They also have great importance for the region because in the lowlands the land is fertile and the loam and clay supply the basic materials for the potteries in Baix Empordà. Baix Empordà is one of four *comarcas* on the Costa Brava, roughly equivalent to the English counties. The others are Alt Empordà in the north, Girona in the interior and La Selva in the south.

The Costa Brava enjoys a prevailing moderate climate. The summers are hot, the winters mild, and there is little rain. However, a shadow is cast on this idyllic climate by the *tramontana*. This stormy wind sweeps down from the Pyrenees, rattles the fishing boats and gnaws at people's nerves. Fortunately it moves on after a few days.

The sea has cut into this land, nibbling away and taking large bites out. What remains are countless rugged bays, some so sheltered that natural harbours have been

Barcelona stimulates both economy and culture

1914
First regional government with limited self-determination

1931
Francesc Macià declares the Catalan Republic. Catalan is the official language

1936
Start of the Spanish Civil War

1939
Catalonia falls to the Fascists and is suppressed by the Franco regime

1977
After Franco's death Catalonia attains autonomy. Catalan is the official language once again

created. The first settlers found the coastline ideal: they had access to the sea and its fishing grounds and were able to build shipyards and ships; maritime trading routes were opened up and they could escape from pirate attacks by retreating to the hilly hinterland.

The first settlers were the Iberians some 7000 years ago and their settlements are the cradle of Spanish civilization. They were followed by the Greeks, Romans and Visigoths. Later there were other influences from the Moorish south of Spain and from northern Europe. This gave rise to a mixture which has left its indelible mark on Catalan culture to this day. Lots of traces of the past are still evident: such as the ancient Iberian settlement of Ullastret, the Roman town of Empúries or the many medieval castles, fortified churches and monasteries.

> **First destination for mass tourism in Spain in the 1950s**

It was also the Costa Brava which became the first destination in Spain when mass tourism took off. At the start of the 1950s the first tourists came from northern and central Europe. Sun, beaches and low prices at first attracted only a few thousand. But every year more and more arrived and set in motion a building boom on the coast. This was when renowned hotel structures and tourist centers such as Platja d'Aro and Lloret de Mar were created and it is these places people have in mind when they think of the Costa Brava. What some see as the ideal destination for the holiday of their dreams – cheap, loud and fun with entertainment readily available – arouses in others a deep aversion.

In recent years there has been a change in the tourist infrastructure on the Costa Brava and, most noticeably, in the attitudes of the tourist service providers, which is gradually attracting a new kind of tourism with a greater emphasis on quality. However, mass tourism still retains its place, with endless hotels lining the beaches, restaurants offering cheap and basic food, and a tourist hubbub that disturbs the holiday idyll.

But the change is noticeable (albeit slow), especially where wellness, family, and nature and wildlife holidays are concerned. And it is with food that the greatest increase in quality is to be seen. Since Ferran Adrià's 'molecular gastronomy' and his restaurant El Bulli (now closed) became a legend, lots of cooking collectives led by

1992 Olympic Games held in Barcelona

2006 Adoption of a new autonomy for Catalonia

2010 Snowstorms over the Costa Brava lead to power cuts and nationwide travel chaos

2011 Government elections in Spain: the conservative PP achieves a majority

2013 Catalonian parliament votes overwhelmingly in favour of regional sovereignty. The Spanish government appeals the declaration

Craggy cliffs and deep blue sea: on the wild, rugged coast at Tossa de Mar

new creative chefs have been set up. They adhere to the tradition of *mar i muntanya (sea and mountains)* cuisine, using local produce and are creating a real renaissance in authentic Catalonian cuisine.

In Spain the Catalans have the image of being decent, hardworking and efficient, but excessively thrifty. They are also seen as withdrawn. Their temperament has nothing in common with the easygoing

The Catalans are considered withdrawn

nature of their fellow countrymen in the south of Spain. And, indeed, the resorts on the Costa Brava are well maintained, the shops well stocked, the staff friendly, willing and able. But beyond the business interactions with tourists they like to keep to themselves.

Catalonia has again acquired a greater degree of independence in the period since Franco. The customs which were forbidden under Franco can today be practised again and the Catalans are once more allowed to speak their own language.

From an economic perspective, the region is strong, creating the greater part of the total Spanish gross domestic product. And of course it is the people too who characterise the landscape between sea and mountains. Whether fishermen, farmers, businessmen or shepherds, they are united by a common love of their homeland and their culture. When Catalans are together and are conversing in *Català,* their own language, you can feel their sense of connection to their country – a country full of beauty with lots of possibilities for a relaxing holiday on the 'wild coast'.

WHAT'S HOT

1 Life is sweet

Patisseries The sweet creations of Xano Saguer are true works of art. The man from Figueres began his career at *Candycash (www.candycash-sa.com)* where amateurs can also learn the art of sugarcraft. Today he is teaching the next generation the art of dessert making at the *Espai Sucre (Carrer Sant Pere més alt, 72, Barcelona, photo)*. You can sample the creations in the restaurant *Espai Sucre (Carrer de la Princesa, 53, Barcelona)*. Another sweet location is *Papabubble (Carrer Ample, 28, Barcelona)*.

Speed & goals

2

Futsal The Spanish also live out their love of football indoors – with *futsal*. When the *Penya Barcelonista Futsal Cup (www.copapenyabarcelonista.es, photo)* or the *Costa Brava Cup (www.costabravacup.es)* are held in Tordera, the streets are empty and everyone is inside at the *Club Futbol Tordera (CF Tordera, Ctra. de l'estació, s/n, Tordera)* to watch the exciting indoor football. Information on the matches at *www.futsal.cat* (but only in Catalan!).

3 A fine thing

Diving centre Sea bass and barracudas, magnificent corals and lots of caves and grottos are there to be explored off the coast. To keep the Costa Brava the diving paradise it is, *Kenna Eco Diving (Passatge Clavell, 9, L'Escala, www.kenna ecodiving.net)* regularly organises dives and workshops on underwater topics. Those who know the sea want to protect it and this is also the credo of *Poseidon Nemrod (Platja Port Pelegri, Calella de Palafrugell)* who offer regular seminars and excursions related to marine ecology.

New tables from old glass

Recycle Barcelona is the capital of the art of recycling. Here Imanol Ossa *(www.imanolossa.com)* makes lamps out of piano keys and lampshades from recycled glass. And he is so successful that restaurants such as *Atmosphère (Carrer Venus, 1–3, Barcelona)* and the *Nice Things (Carrer Girona, 6, Figueres)* chain of shops are decorated with his lamps. And Imanol Ossa is not the only one on trend. *Ciclus (near Flow, Carrer Gran de Gràcia, 188, Barcelona, photo)* creates well conceived furniture from recycled bottles such as the coffee table which can also be used as a vase. And it is not only in Barcelona that resources are recycled. For example, at the huge flower festival in Girona more and more flowers are displayed in nets woven from plastic bags or in old wine bottles.

4

The man & the sea

Pesca-tourism Mending nets, maintaining course, sorting the catch – there is nothing romantic about the work of a fisherman. Those who want to have hands-on experience of the fishing life, go to *Yumping (www.yumping.com)* where the staff organise day trips on board genuine fishing boats in Port de la Selva. *Escapada de Pesca (escapadadepesca.com)* organises not only classic boat trips, but also trips with genuine old seafarers. And because an early start is essential, the company works closely with the boutique hotel *Hostal Sa Rascassa (Cala d'Aiguafreda, 3, Begur)* and, for practical reasons, the 'fishermen for a day' are collected straight from the breakfast table.

5

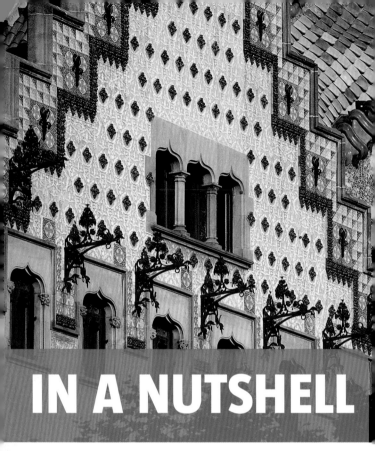

IN A NUTSHELL

BEACHES

It is the beaches on the Costa Brava which are the main attraction for most visitors. There are 119 officially listed beaches between the French border in the north and Blanes in the south. Some are only small bays, romantic coves protected by pine trees growing down to the sea, whilst others are sandy beaches miles long; some are close to fishing villages, and others line the front of the major resorts. For the most part the beaches have fine sand and are cleaned every morning by the local community. Nowadays all the official beaches are equipped with showers, and private companies rent out loungers and run small beach bars. The beaches usually have a very gentle slope down into the water, so children and the elderly should have no difficulties. The relevant flags show the water quality, the current weather and the degree of danger.

CASINO

Some Spanish *casinos* are not places where games of chance are played. Every community of any size makes a building available for its senior citizens where they can spend the day. They sit together, chat, play cards and read the paper. Feast days are also celebrated on the premises and a bar provides visitors with food and drink.

Photo: Buildings by Antoni Gaudí

Human towers and gigantic patron saints: learn more about Catalan art and culture, ceramics, cork and circle dances

The *casino* is open to the public and anyone can pop in. For tourists it can be an interesting experience to immerse themselves in the daily life of the locals. Some of these *casinos* are housed in historic buildings and are correspondingly well equipped, such as in Sant Feliu de Guíxols or Palafrugell. One more thing: the concept *casino* meaning a day centre, is not current throughout Spain.

CASTELLERS

This word derives from the Catalan *castell,* meaning castle. The *castellers* build human towers as a reflection of Catalan national pride. On national holidays young people, dressed in Catalan traditional costume and accompanied by the beat of drums, get together on a square and form a circle by holding one another's shoulders. A second group, reduced by two or three people, climbs on to this foundation circle, then another and another until the smallest member is standing at a dizzying height right on the top. And he can be sure of rapturous applause from the spectators. Good *castellers* can build a tower up to eight levels, and the record stands at ten.

CATALAN

The Catalans have always spoken their own language, which they nurture with great seriousness. The use of *Català* in public was banned under Franco. When democracy was re-introduced and Catalonia achieved autonomy, they began with ever greater resolve to teach and speak their own language in schools, offices and at the university – in addition to Spanish which continues to dominate on the Costa Brava. The Catalan spellings are mainly used in this guide.

CAVA

As Champagne is to the French, so Cava is to the Spanish and especially the Catalans, though for legal reasons it may not be called Champagne. Some, and not only Catalans, claim that Cava is almost the same as Champagne, but better – and

it is certainly cheaper! Cava has been produced by traditional methods since about 1860. Grapes are grown throughout Catalonia, but to be used for Cava they must be sourced from registered vineyards. The centre of Cava production is Sant Sadurní d'Anoia in Penedès. In 2001 for the first time, more Cava was bought worldwide than Champagne.

CERAMICS

Catalan ceramics prospered in the Middle Ages. The green and violet motifs – dancers, gardens of paradise and animals – were originally taken up by the Moors, but the requisite skills later developed a strong independence in Catalonia. Motifs such as courtly scenes and flowers in cobalt blue became all the fashion and ceramics were exported as far as Italy. The centre of ceramics production was Bisbal, where you can still find today very nice pieces and, in fact, as you drive into the town, huge flower pots, floor tiles in thousands of colours and figures of all shapes and sizes are displayed on either side of the main road. However, production there is now rather limited, most ceramic items coming from the south of Spain.

Excavations in Empúries have revealed the remains of a Greek settlement

COOKERY COLLECTIVES

In 1995, after the 2nd Congress of Catalan Cuisine, cookery collectives were established with chefs playing an important role. The aim was, and still is, to promote local produce and biodiversity and to put a stop to the trend of all food being the same. To promote high quality tourism not only are restaurants and agriculture involved, but also every aspect of the tourist trade. The cookery collectives are therefore exclusive associations with high standards of professional ethics and product quality. Only restaurants which satisfy these self-imposed demands are accepted as members of a cookery collective, of which there are now eight on the Costa Brava, with more seeking to join all the time.

CORK

Thousands of families once earned their living from *suro,* cork. The cork industry developed in the 17th century, up to 1900 no fewer than 13,000 workers were employed in 615 factories, manufacturing cork products such as bottle seals, shoes, wallpapers and fishing materials. The centre of the cork industry was Palafrugell where there are still a few factories. Today cork production in Catalonia occupies third position in the whole of Europe after Portugal and Andalusia.

DALÍ

In addition to Joan Miró and Antoni Tàpies, Salvador Dalí (1904–89) is the most important painter in Catalonia. He was born in Figueres, went for a time to Paris, but lived mainly in Catalonia. You can gain an idea of the surrealist artist's eccentric life by visiting the Dalí Museum in Figueres and in his summer house in Cadaqués. Dalí was a controversial figure because of his lifestyle and his acceptance of the Franco regime. But it has to be said he brought a lot of positive benefits to Cadaqués: because Dalí threatened to move away, no large hotel buildings were erected there. And, of course, the town also has him to thank for its present popularity with tourists.

FISHING

In addition to tourism, fishing is still the main source of income for the local population, even though it is very much in decline. Anchovies, monkfish, sardines, crayfish, crabs, swordfish and mackerel are caught by line, trap and net and are then auctioned in the *La Llotjá* hall. But beware: not all the fish served in restaurants is caught off the local coast. Places with major fishing fleets are Palamós, Llançà, Roses, Blanes and l'Escala.

GAUDÍ

Antoni Gaudí is arguably the most famous architect not only in Catalonia, but throughout Spain. The representative of *modernismo,* Spanish Art Nouveau, was born in Reus, Tarragona in 1852. He has left a legacy of cave-like balconies and house facades throughout Catalonia. Countless buildings in Barcelona bear witness to his creativity and the still unfinished Sagrada Familia cathedral is his most grandiose work. Gaudí died impoverished in 1926 after a road traffic accident.

GEGANTS

At every funfair, at every feast day in honour of a patron saint, they make their appearance, usually as a pair: the *gegants*. Almost 5m/16ft tall, made from papier mâché, wire and strips of wood, with funnily shaped heads, they totter through the crowds entertaining the people, but also preventing the religious processions appearing too solemn. For this reason, therefore, for a long time the church imposed a ban on the figures, whose origin can probably be traced back to 17th century Mallorca. After making their appearance the giants vanish once more into the community's storerooms or are exhibited in museums, such as the Can Quintana Museum in Torroella de Montgrí.

GREEKS

In about 600 BC the Greeks founded settlements throughout the Mediterranean area. They arrived in Catalonia from present day France, and places such as Roses and Empúries date back to the Greeks. The Greeks also introduced wine growing and the planting of olive groves.

IBERIANS

The Iberians came from Africa and settled on the Iberian Peninsula in the 4th millennium BC, reaching northern Spain in 700 BC. They are considered to be the original inhabitants of Catalonia. The settlement at Ullastret is evidence of their culture.

JEWS

The first Jewish families settled on the Costa Brava in Girona around 890 BC. They lived in the *call*, their own part of the town, characterised by narrow streets with multi-storey buildings; small gardens and hidden courtyards; and synagogues in the immediate vicinity. The Jews enjoyed autonomy from the local town government and tax concessions, which caused constant hostility towards them, especially from the Catholic Church. After much persecution they were expelled by royal decree in 1492. What remained were the so-called Jewish quarters, such as in La Bisbal.

MIRÓ

Joan Miró (1893–1983) was born in Barcelona and is one of the great surrealist painters. He was a friend of Picasso's, lived for a time in Paris, but returned to Barcelona where he created the Miró Foundation, a museum which now exhibits important works by him as well as promoting and publicising the work of contemporary artists.

MODERNISM

Modernism (in Spanish, *modernismo*) is an art movement which arose towards the end of the 19th century and relates to other art forms, such as sculpture, poetry, theatre and painting, and not just architecture. This is an art movement which was known in other countries by the name Art Nouveau. The forms of expression are playful, asymmetrical, with sweeping curves and decorated with flower-like ornamentations. It is reflected in many materials and designs: in building facades, wrought iron railings, portals and window frames. But *modernismo* is also to be seen in objects made of glass, metal, silver, gold, wood and ceramics. The art movement is apparent throughout Spain. On the Costa Brava there is architectural evidence in Caldes de Malavella, Figueres, Girona and Lloret de Mar and elsewhere.

PLA

The most important writer in Catalonia was Josep Pla, a man who chronicled his homeland in precise detail. He was born in Palafrugell in 1897 and after the Spanish Civil War was forced to write in Spanish. He became well-known for his critical newspaper articles and travel reports about Catalonia and Mallorca. He died in 1947 in Llofriu. In the house where Pla was born, less than a mile away in Palafrugell, there is now a museum commemorating him.

RAMBLAS

These wide promenades are to be found in all the major towns and resorts on the Costa Brava. The *rambla* is where it all happens in the evening. People flirt, enjoy an evening drink or simply sit and people

Barcelona's vibrant Las Ramblas promenade is ideal for a stroll, people watching and shopping

watch, and there can be spontaneous *sardana* dancing. Most of the *ramblas* follow the course of former river beds and the most famous is the *rambla* in Barcelona.

RIVALRIES

Which football team is better: *Barça* or *Real Madrid?* Where's the best place to live, here or there? These and similar questions characterise the rivalry between Catalonia and the rest of Spain. The independence of the Catalans was strengthened in the Statute of Autonomy passed in 2006. In addition to the right to their own language, this also brought greater independence in many areas such as education, health, civil law, environment, transport, commerce and public safety, and Catalonia has its own police force. The rivalries remain: when a group consists of both Catalans and Spanish, the Catalans will deliberately speak Catalan, knowing that most Spanish people will not understand. And Catalan government spokespersons often give their answers in Catalan when interviewed on Spanish television.

SARDANA

This ancient Catalan dance, the epitome of Catalan identity, is danced in a circle with all the participants holding hands. The orchestra is dominated by the *tenora*, a sort of oboe. At first two dancers take short and then long dance steps towards an imaginary centre of the circle, gradually being joined by other dancers. The *sardana* is danced at festivals and also spontaneously or regularly on town squares, as in Figueres for example.

TÀPIES

Antoni Tàpies was a painter born in Barcelona in 1923 and was one of the best-known representatives of the Catalan avant-garde after the Second World War. Despite censorship by the Spanish authorities, he managed to use his paintings to protest against political suppression in his homeland. There is a foundation in Barcelona dedicated to him *(www.funda ciotapies.org)*. Today Tàpies is considered one of Spain's most important contemporary artists.

FOOD & DRINK

The regional Catalan cuisine on the Costa Brava is characterised by a fusion of the produce available from the sea, mountains and local agriculture. What you eat in this region is very much dependent on where you eat.

Inland it is meat, poultry and vegetables which are eaten, but on the coast it is mainly fish which is served. The rocky coast provides various fish and seafood such as sardines, bream, mackerel, and all sorts of shellfish, crayfish, prawns, calamari and monkfish.

Catalonian agriculture produces poultry, rice, peppers, artichokes, pumpkins, garlic, almonds, aubergines, beans, courgettes, onions and tomatoes, whilst the woods are rich in game and mushrooms. Given this abundance it is no surprise that, in the course of time, these ingredients have been used to create some really unusual dishes which have nowadays been refined with modern methods and a new awareness.

Some culinary specialities of the region would seem, given their simplicity, to be derived from the eating habits of poor people, but they are nonetheless delicious. Such as *pa amb tomàquet,* toasted bread rubbed with garlic and topped with tomato, served with almost every meal. Another popular side dish is *allioli,* which

From land and sea: vegetables, mushrooms, meat and fish are combined in the Costa Brava kitchens to create unusual dishes

means nothing more than garlic and oil, but is served in all sorts of variations, even as a mayonnaise.

The *escalivadas* are grilled vegetables, preferably onions and peppers, steeped in olive oil and eaten cold. Another speciality is **INSIDER TIP** *suquet*, a thick fish stew with beans or peas and potatoes, once the staple meal for fishermen. On board it was usually served with a thick slice of bread; now it is often made using ingredients such as saffron and almonds. *Zarzuela* is actually a term for Spanish operetta, but in this case it is another fish stew, this time made with whatever vegetables are currently available from the local market. A rather more refined fish dish is *rape Costa Brava*, monkfish grilled with prawns and eaten cold with a fresh salad.

LOCAL SPECIALITIES

▶ **Almejas con alubias** – clams with beans –clams steamed in a little oil and deglazed with white wine and then cooked in fish stock with beans

▶ **Arroz negro a la cazuela** – rice with squid, eel, garlic, oil, tomatoes and onions – the ingredients are sautéd and thensteamed mussels and rice are then added, the squid ink turns everything black

▶ **Bacalao** – dried fish, frequently cod, is also called *peixopalo* on the Costa Brava – it is served for example with a tomato and garlic sauce

▶ **Berenjenas rellenos** – aubergines filled with pork *(came de cerdo)*

▶ **Habas catalanas** – beans cooked with diced bacon, simple and tasty

▶ **Mongetes amb botifarra** – beans and *botifarra,* a hard or sweet sausage, depending on the area

▶ **Pa amb tomàquet** – toasted bread topped with garlic and tomato (photo right)

▶ **Pimientos rellenos** – stuffed peppers – often with rice, but also with pork and squid, an especially spicy combination

▶ **Sanfaina** – aubergines, courgettes, onions, tomatoes and garlic are cooked to a pulp and served as vegetable sauce to accompany potato dishes

▶ **Sardinas a la plancha** – grilled sardines – seasoned with garlic and parsley, are an essential component of *sardinera,* a sardine dish (photo left)

▶ **Zarzuela** – fish stew, usually made with *merluza,* hake, steamed with vegetables, clams, prawns and garlic. It should, of course, be accompanied by *pa amb tomàquet*

For dessert *crema catalana,* a type of crème caramel, is very popular. Or try out the local cheese varieties, such as *recuit,* a soft fresh cheese made from sheep's milk. There are plenty of local wines to choose from to complement all main dishes, the main producer being Comarca Girona who make white, rosé and red wines. Not to mention the sparkling *Cava,* the Catalan sparkling wine, which is not only enjoyed at celebrations. A regional speciality is *garnatxa,* a sweet wine.

In addition to the coffees which are readily available in Spain such as *con leche* (with milk), *solo* (espresso) and *carajillo* (with rum or brandy), on the Costa Brava there is a speciality: *cremat*. A social drink of hot rum with some sugar, a few coffee beans, lemon peel and a fresh cinnamon stick, traditionally a winter warmer.

If you are feeling peckish between meals, then there is *merienda*, a word which keeps cropping up in Spain. It describes a small dish, larger than tapas but less than a full meal. Cervantes raved about the 'pots with aubergines and pieces of rabbit' in one of his poems. More recently it was often also a piece of bread with chocolate which could take the edge off your hunger. But today there are no limits as to what it can comprise, and on the Costa Brava the *merienda* can be a small plate of sardines or a few mussels. And a *copa* (glass of wine) is included.

Compared with the *merienda*, things are very different on the Costa Brava as far as tapas is concerned. In central Spain free appetisers are provided with the drinks, this isn't something which happens in Catalonia. *Tapar* means to 'cover'. There was a time when the glass was covered with a small plate to guard against insects – a custom which is no longer observed today. Tapas are now mainly served as side dishes to complement the drinks and they have to be ordered and paid for. In tapas bars *montaditos* are also often provided, small snacks comprising a piece of cheese, an anchovy or ham, piled or skewered with a toothpick on a piece of bread.

Eating habits are different from those in central Europe, with people eating much later: lunch is not before 1pm and as late as 3pm; in the evenings dinner is from 9pm, though in the tourist resorts restaurants will accommodate their guests' habits and serve earlier. If you are famished, you can snack in a tapas bar before the official serving times.

The hotels in the average price category do not, on the whole, serve their foreign guests sophisticated local cuisine. They tend to adapt to their guests and serve what they think the guest would normally eat at home. This applies especially for hotels catering for package tourists. If you

Popular dessert: *crema catalana*, a vanilla dessert with a caramel topping

really want to try out authentic local cuisine, then you should seek out a bar, restaurant or hotel where Catalan food is on offer and where the locals also eat.

If you want a substantial breakfast in the morning, then you are best off with the buffet in your hotel: a Spanish breakfast in a bar consists only of coffee and croissant.

SHOPPING

The tourist centres on the Costa Brava have a wide range of souvenirs. Costume jewellery, printed T-shirts, mass-produced arts and crafts and the inevitable *botas*, cheaply made leather wallets, are all popular. And then there are the street hawkers selling Chinese silk scarves, African wood carvings and pirated CDs.

One special feature you will come across shopping on the Costa Brava: in many shops there is a ticket machine – you take a number and wait until it is called out. If there is no machine, then it is best to ask where the queue ends – with the words: *Quien es el ultimo?* (Who is last?). This will prevent any misunderstandings.

BOOKS & GRAPHIC WORKS

In the book shops you will find a wide range of literature about the Costa Brava, especially illustrated books. There are also some biographies of the great local artists such as Salvador Dalí. You can buy Dalí graphics in Barcelona, Figueres, Girona and Cadaqués.

CERAMICS

Around La Bisbal you will find wickerwork and lovely ceramics from coffee sets to flower pots to complete dinner services. As you drive into the town you will pass one ceramics shop after another, however, only very few ceramics are now produced directly in Bisbal, most come from other regions of Spain. The authentic Bisbal colours are brown and green.

KITCHEN APPLIANCES

The *ferreterias*, hardware stores, are a treasure trove of rather curious kitchen utensils and appliances. Here you can get relatively cheap *aceitera*, the popular olive oil cans made of stainless metal, or paella pans available in various sizes. At the markets and also in the hardware shops you will find bowls carved from olive wood, cutlery, containers and chopping boards.

LOCAL PRODUCE

The best place to buy authentic regional produce is in the villages of the hinterland

Food and ceramics: to avoid mass produced items, you should skip the coastal resorts and browse for local products inland

where the locals do their shopping. At the weekly markets lots of produce from the local farms is sold, such as olives, sausages, honey, chestnuts and cheese. The town *bodegas* sell local wine, *cava* (sparkling wine), brandy and liqueurs, which are cheaper than in the rest of Europe. Gourmets like to shop in Llançà, the main port, for anchovies and potted anchovies – they are considerably cheaper than elsewhere. When shopping in the indoor markets, do not be tempted to touch the beautifully arranged mountains of fruit: the stallholders will on the whole react somewhat indignantly.

cially in Barcelona there are the popular *Camper* and *Pikolinos brands*.

Alpargatas, known in France by the name *espadrilles,* are a Catalan speciality: once a pauper shoe with uppers made of canvas and soles made of esparto grass, today they are available in much better materials and in every colour. In addition to many no-name brands there is also one famous brand selling a more refined version: *Campesina* made by *Castañer*, a family-run company founded in 1927 with a workshop dating back to 1776, when the first espadrille maker Rafael Castañer was born.

SHOES

For a long time now shoes in Spain have not been as cheap as they were just ten years ago. Nevertheless, there is a wider selection on the Costa Brava, and espe-

TOBACCO PRODUCTS

Smokers can get their money's worth in *éstancos,* tobacconists, where they can find INSIDER TIP Cuban cigars, for example, up to 20 per cent cheaper than in the UK.

THE PERFECT ROUTE

TO THE THERMAL BATHS

Thanks to the absence of mass tourism, ① *Tossa de Mar* → p. 79 has been able to retain its very own charm, characterised by peace and quiet and an unobtrusive holiday atmosphere. The town is your starting point for setting off into the interior. Soon the GI681 country road winds its way higher and higher via numerous hair-pin bends, with cork oak woods lining both sides of the road. After about 20km/12mi you reach the town of Llagostera where you turn off westwards, to ② *Caldes de Malavella* → p. 76 a further 8km/5mi along. The Romans used the hot springs here and you should sample the famous healing waters in the Balneario Vichy Catalán.

MEGALITHIC DOLMEN

Returning via Llagostera you come to ③ *Santa Cristina d'Aro* → p. 66 with its restored railway station dating from the time of the cork boom and now houses the Font Picant restaurant. Here you leave the busy C35 and head north via the narrow GIV6612 to reach ④ *Dolmen de la Cova d'en Daina* → p. 60, a megalithic grave some 4000 years old. Via Calonge after about 15km/10mi you come to ⑤ *Palamós* → p. 57 where you can enjoy a lunch of fresh fish in the Club Nautic.

BLUE WATER

Via the busy C31 you are soon in ⑥ *Palafrugell* → p. 60 (photo left), once the centre of the cork industry. If you are not keen on visiting the cork museum, then there is only one thing: you must go down to the sea again. Via *Tamariu* → p. 54 you come to the pretty ⑦ *Bay of Aiguaxelida,* a good place for a break and a swim. Refreshed, you return via Palafrugell and then ⑧ *Pals* → p. 54 (photo right) for about another 13km/9mi to the medieval village of ⑨ *Peratallada* → p. 56.

RUINS AND SMALL FISH

Just a few miles further on lies ⑩ *Ciutat Iberica d'Ullastret* → p. 56 where you can explore the excavations of a pre-historic town. ⑪ *Torroella de Montgrí* → p. 66 is the nearest town of any size, where it is worth sampling the local cuisine in the Can Carcan. A detour takes you to ⑫ *L'Estartit* → p. 69, where diving fans might well be tempted by the water sports centre to take a longer break. Returning through a relatively flat landscape without any outstanding features, ⑬ *L'Escala* → p. 41 is the next port of call, a busy town with a fishing port renowned for its salted and cured anchovies which you can buy everywhere.

DALÍ IN FIGUERES AND CADAQUÉS

You can now make rapid progress on the excellent C31 road to (14) *Figueres* → p. 38. Before you start to explore the world of Dalí, leave your car in a car park because there is no chance of finding a free parking space here. It is 20km/12mi to (15) *Roses* → p. 46 which is always busy, with the bay crowded with holidaymakers. It is much calmer in (16) *Cadaqués* → p. 32 and in the local *casino* you can enjoy a good coffee and consider whether you now want to pay a visit to Dalí's summer house or have a stroll through the Cap de Creus nature park. In any event, it is worth driving to (17) *Cap de Creus* → p. 37 because from there, the most easterly point on the Costa Brava, you can enjoy a stunning view.

FINAL STOP PORTBOU

Via a narrow, winding road you drive to (18) *El Port de la Selva* → p. 44, an idyllic port with some good seafood restaurants. Refreshed, you can now make another detour into the mountains above the town. This is where the former monastery (19) *Sant Pere de Rodes* → p. 45 is situated, commanding a fantastic view of the coast as far as the foothills of the Pyrenees. Back on the main road, you head north on the very busy, winding N260 which leads to the French border and to (20) *Portbou* → p. 45 with its famous border station.

Approx. 270km/170mi
Actual driving time approx. 6 hours
Recommended length of trip: 2 days
Detailed map of the route on the back cover, in the road atlas and the pull-out map

ALT EMPORDÀ

If you approach from the Pyrenees, you will first encounter a rugged landscape: bleak mountains, often crowned with fortresses, and villages nestling in valleys with rough stone houses and barren land.

And then there is the coast. This too is rugged, in keeping with the Costa Brava name. Steep cliffs tower above the breakers, the sea having left deep scars in the land. Only when you arrive here do you become aware of the area's special charm. The water in the bays is clear and blue and fragrant pine woods provide shade. The sea reflects the white of the villages, where women sit mending and

fishermen play dominos in smoke-filled bars even though smoking in public places is now banned. If you want to experience the Costa Brava away from the hustle and bustle of tourism, then the north is the perfect place for you – provided you avoid the most obvious tourist centres.

CADAQUÉS

(121 F4) (*Ⓜ H4*) ★ ● **Cadaqués is a refreshingly pleasant place. It is so much calmer here than in the tourist centres on the Costa Brava, even if there are**

Castles and mountains, sea and sand – the wild north – where you can hike on stony paths and swim in crystal clear bays

sparkling yachts lying at anchor in the extensive bay.

Whilst there are now only a few inhabitants who earn their living from fishing, visitors can nonetheless find here what romantics would call a 'fishing village'. There are boats bobbing up and down in the bay, the town centre is not dominated by hotel buildings, and it is not only tourists who are to be seen in the town's narrow streets lined with whitewashed houses.

When you hear the name Cadaqués, you may immediately think of Salvador Dalí, the famous and controversial surrealist painter. This was where he had his summer house and where he invited the great artists of his time, from Federico García Lorca to Paul Eluard to Gabriel García Márquez.

The village of Cadaqués with its beach, white buildings, narrow streets and church

SIGHTSEEING

ESGLÉSIA PARROQUIAL

The parish church towers up over the town centre, an image which you see again and again on many postcards and paintings. It was destroyed in 1543 by Algerian pirates and rebuilt in the 16th century. The Baroque altar inside, carved by the Catalan Pau Costa in 1727, is worth seeing. From the churchyard you look out over the roofs of the town. *Wed, Sat, Sun 8pm | town centre*

MUSEU DE CADAQUÉS

The museum situated in the town centre is dedicated to Salvador Dalí. But its success also derives from the surprising range of its temporary exhibitions of works by artists associated with the village such as Pichot, Niebla and Picasso. It also has a small collection of paintings by mainly Catalan artists. *Daily 10am–1pm and 3pm–8pm | admission 5 euros | Carrer Narcís Monturiol, 15*

FOOD & DRINK

INSIDER TIP BAR CAP DE CREUS

You can enjoy a fantastic view of the sea from the easternmost point in Spain, high up on Cap de Creus. This restaurant exudes all the charm of a smoke-filled bar (in spite of the public smoking ban) and serves good traditional food as well as Indian curries. *Daily | Cap de Creus, s/n | tel. 972 19 90 05 | Budget*

ES BALUARD

There is a great view of the Bay of Cadaqués. Fish tops the bill in this restaurant, the paella is worthy of a special mention, and the homemade desserts, such as INSIDER TIP sheep's milk yogurt with blueberries, are both interesting and delicious. *Closed Wed | Riba Nemesi Llorens, 2 | tel. 9 72 15 93 45 | Expensive*

ES RACÓ
There is a panoramic view of the port from the large, elevated ☆ dining room. Fish and traditional Catalan food are served. *Daily | Carrer del Dr. Callís, 3 | tel. 9 72 15 94 80 | Budget*

SHOPPING

There are numerous art shops and galleries, selling primarily reproductions of works by Dalí and Picasso, as well as craftwork from pottery to costume jewellery.

CAN SALÒ
This well stocked ceramics shop sells artistic items and classic Spanish ceramics for everyday use. *Passeig, 12*

GALERIA NORD-EST
Objets d'art, paintings and books are sold here, and there are also temporary exhibitions by contemporary artists. *Carrer Pianc, 2*

WEEKLY MARKET
Fresh fruit and vegetables, Catalan cheese and cold meat as well as lots of everyday items are sold here. *Mon 8am–2pm in the Riera, the dried river bed*

SPORTS, ACTIVITIES & BEACHES

The beaches are small and stony and the town beach is usually crowded. Lots of bays are hard to get to, some only by boat. If you do not mind walking, you will find small bays with clear water all round Cap de Creus.

BOAT TRIP TO CAP DE CREUS
In good weather there are daily trips at midday, 4pm and 6pm from Es Poal, the port of Cadaqués. *Creuers Cadaqués Es Poal, s/n | tel. 9 72 15 94 62 | www.creuers cadaques.cat*

★ **Cadaqués**
Fishing village with white-washed houses, original village centre, narrow streets, a beach with a short promenade in the village and lots of atmosphere → p. 32

★ **Parc Natural del Cap de Creus**
Nature reserve with a wild landscape, secluded bays, lovely hiking trails, with steep drops and surrounding rocks → p. 37

★ **Port Lligat with Dalí Museum**
Salvador Dalí and his wife Gala lived on this small bay → p. 37

★ **Teatro Museo Dalí**
Colourful fantasies by Dalí – this is a must for lovers of his art. The museum in Figueres (Dalí's birthplace) attracts thousands of visitors from all over the world every year → p. 38

★ **Museu del Castell de Peralada**
80,000 books are just one highlight of the museum of a former industrialist with collections which once belonged to the Catalan upper classes → p. 41

★ **Parc Natural dels Aiguamolls de l'Empordà**
Lots of migratory birds make a stop in the wetlands of this nature reserve → p. 49

MARCO POLO HIGHLIGHTS

BOAT HIRE

Kayaking Costa Brava | kiosk on Port Lligat bay | tel. 6 46 90 15 88 | www.kayakingcostabrava.com

DIVING

Sotamar | Avenida Caritat Serinyana, 17 | all year | tel. 9 72 25 88 76 | www.sotamar.com

ENTERTAINMENT

INSIDER TIP ▶ CASINO DE CADAQUÉS

This is a pleasant meeting place: nice people, not too loud, good discreet service. Large windows fill the place with light and provide a view of the people strolling past outside. Internet café with pool table. *Plaça de Tremols, 1*

LA HABANA

The boss himself now and again takes up his guitar in this cosy bar. *C/Doctor Bartomeus, 2*

WHERE TO STAY

HOTEL OCTAVIA

This is a relatively new hotel in the town centre with bright, cheery furnishings. *41 rooms | Riera Sant Vicenç, s/n | tel. 9 72 15 92 25 | www.hoteloctavia.net | Moderate*

HOTEL ROCAMAR

This is situated a little out of the town but nonetheless still within walking distance of Cadaqués bay. It is quiet, some rooms have a view of the sea and there is a sauna. *70 rooms | Carrer Virgen del Carmen, s/n | tel. 9 72 25 81 50 | www.rocamar.com | Expensive*

L'HOSTALET DE CADAQUÉS

This relatively new hotel close to the centre, near the central car park, is good value for money. *8 rooms | Carrer Miquel Rosset, 13 | tel. 9 72 25 82 06 | www.hostalet cadaques.com | Budget*

INFORMATION

OFICINA MUNICIPAL DE TURISME
Carrer Cotxe, 2 | tel. 9 72 25 83 15 | www.cadaques.cat

WHERE TO GO

FAR DE CALA NANS ☼
(121 F4) (*ω H4*)

The lighthouse above the Bay of Nans lies some 3km/2mi south-east of the town centre. You can start off by car but then you get to the end of the town and can drive no further. Here is an easy footpath (past bathing bays you can climb down to) which takes you to the lighthouse. From here you can enjoy a wonderful extended view of the coast and sea.

PARC NATURAL DEL CAP DE CREUS ⭐
(121 E–F 3–5) (*G–H 4–5*)

This is where the Pyrenees come to an end. The park comprises an area which takes in almost the whole peninsula between El Port de La Selva and Roses. In the mountains there are numerous, well signposted hiking trails at all levels of difficulty. They lead through a wild, partly barren landscape with precipitous drops to the sea and there are stony paths which offer no protection from the wind. There is little vegetation apart from low shrubs and gorse. Other hiking trails lead to the bays of Cap de Creus. The park office has a wide range of information and free maps are available. It is situated in the old Sant Pere de Rodes Monastery (approx. 18km/11mi from Cadaqués). *Office opening times: June–Sept daily 10am–2pm and 4pm–7pm, Oct–May 10am–2pm and 3pm–5.30pm | tel. 9 72 19 31 91 | www.parcsdecatalunya.net*

PORT LLIGAT WITH DALÍ MUSEUM ⭐
(121 F4) (*H4*)

You can get to Port Lligat, 3km/2mi beyond Cadaqués either on foot via a winding coastal path or by car on the country road. This is where Salvador Dalí lived with his wife Gala till her death in 1982. At first all you can see are the eggs on the roof of Dalí's house but, as you get nearer, a small bay opens up with a pier. Rounds trips start from here on board the 'Gala'.

The museum itself has very strict rules for visitors. Only groups of ten people are admitted at the same time and there is a time limit on the tour through Dalí's whimsically furnished living quarters. *Daily mid June–mid Sept 9.30am–9pm, otherwise 10.30am–6pm | admission 10 euros | advance booking is essential | tel. 9 72 25 10 15 | www.salvador-dali.org*

Wild clouds, wild sea: rugged bay in the Parc Natural del Cap de Creus

FIGUERES

MAP ON PAGE 126
(120 B5) (*ld E4–5*) **If it were not for the fact that Salvador Dalí was born here in 1904, Figueres (pop. 35,000) would no doubt be no more than an average small rural town.**

The main town of Alt Empordà is neither particularly attractive, nor are there any interesting sights to explore. But thanks to the Dalí Museum which opened in 1974, the town is now listed in every travel guide and attracts tourists from all over the world.

SIGHTSEEING

CASTELL DE SANT FERRAN
The 18th century fortress was regarded at its time to be the largest military building in Europe. With an area covering 80 acres, it provided accommodation for 6000 soldiers, and almost as many horses could be stabled here. Guided tours are now available after the Castell was comprehensively renovated in 1997. *Daily 10.30am–2pm and 4pm–6pm | admission 3 euros | Carrer Pujada del Castell, s/n*

MUSEU DE L'EMPORDÀ
The museum's collection includes items from the Iberian period, sculptures from the Middle Ages as well as contemporary art, supplemented by loans from the Prado in Madrid. There are also temporary exhibitions. *Tue–Sat 11am–8pm, Sun 11am–2pm | admission 4 euros or included in the admission price of the Dalí Museum | Rambla, 2*

MUSEU DEL JOQUET
The museum has a collection of several thousand toys. But it is not only the individual exhibits which are of interest, but also their previous owners, including Dalí, García Lorca, Joan Miró and other famous figures. *Tue–Sat 10am–7pm, Sun 11am–6pm | admission 6 euros | Sant Pere, 1*

PLAÇA DE L'AJUNTAMENT
The square, laid out in 1757, is situated at the heart of the town. Once the vegetable market used to be held here, today you can relax, away from the traffic, in one of the surrounding cafés opposite the town hall. *Between Carrer Sant Pere and Carrer Girona*

TEATRO MUSEO DALÍ ★ ●
Dalí built his own museum on the ruins of the town theatre destroyed in the Spanish Civil War. The surrealist painter considered his birthplace to be the only fitting place where his extravagant works could be displayed after his death. For him the theatre was also the ideal setting, located opposite the church where he had been baptised. The museum is unique. Huge eggs and a transparent dome crown the roof and inside there is a fascinating labyrinth of rooms, corridors and courtyards. Nowhere else can you see such a

LOW BUDGET

▶ In many places – such as in Portbou and Roses – there are *bodegas* (drinks shops) where you can buy Catalan sparkling wine *(cava)* as well as wine on tap quite reasonably. You can get 1.5L of good local wine for less than 2 euros.

▶ Free Internet access is provided by lots of public libraries and *Casa del Cultura* in Llançà. *Mon–Fri 5pm–9pm, Sat 9am–1pm | Plaça Major*

Teatro Museo Dalí: a labyrinth of rooms, corridors and courtyards behind a classical facade

diversity of Dalí works – a sumptuous treat. In the Dalí Joies side room there is a display of the jewellery items designed by Dalí. *March–June daily 9.30am–6pm, July–Sept daily 9am–8pm, Oct daily 9.30am–6pm, Nov–Feb daily 10.30am–6pm | admission 12 euros | Plaça Gala i Salvador Dalí, 5 | www.salvador-dali.org*

FOOD & DRINK

DURÀN

The Duràn Hotel restaurant in serves food made with fresh, seasonal ingredients. *Daily | Carrer Lasauca, 5 | tel. 9 72 50 12 50 | Expensive*

EMPORDÀ 😊

In this traditional restaurant – which claims to be the cradle of new Catalan cuisine – only fresh local produce is used. It was founded in 1961 by the famous chef Josep Mercader with the project name El Motel. It is not only the restaurant which is famous, the food is also the stuff of legends, such as *el bacallà de Josep Mercader*, charcoal grilled *bacalao* on a bed of spinach. *Daily | Av. Salvador Dalí, 170 | tel. 9 72 50 05 62 | www.hotelemporda.com | Expensive*

LIZARRÁN

You can enjoy *montaditos* (bruschetta) with every possible topping in this tapas bar, and on Thursday they serve paella at a very reasonable price. *Daily | Monturiol, 3 | tel. 9 72 50 66 67 | www.lizarran.es | Budget*

SHOPPING

In *Carrer Girona* and its small side streets there are shops selling clothes, shoes and jewellery. There is a fruit and vegetable market every Tuesday, Thursday and

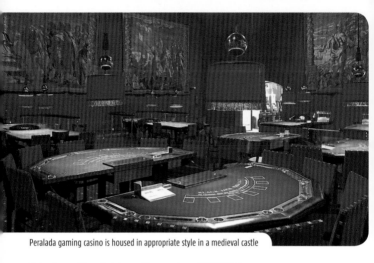

Peralada gaming casino is housed in appropriate style in a medieval castle

Saturday on *Plaça Catalunya*. You can also buy Dalí reproductions in some shops in *Carrer de Sant Pere*.

ENTERTAINMENT

Evenings in Figueres are relatively quiet. There are restaurants and bars open in the evenings in the area around *Carrer Jonquera*.

WHERE TO STAY

DURÀN
Located in the centre of the town, just a few minutes' walk from the Dalí Museum, this hotel has bright, spacious rooms. *65 rooms | Carrer Lasauca, 5 | tel. 972 50 12 50 | www.hotelduran.com | Expensive*

LOS ÁNGELES
This hotel in the old town offers good value for money, with satellite TV, triples for families, air conditioning and restaurant. *39 rooms | Carrer Barceloneta, 10 | tel. 972 51 06 61 | www.hotelangeles.com | Budget*

PIRINEOS
This is a comfortable hotel, with tastefully furnished rooms in shades of brown, located 500m from the Dalí Museum. *56 rooms | Av. Salvador Dalí, 68 | tel.*

SIDORME
Opened in 2008, this hotel just outside the town (towards Roses) offers outstanding value for money. In addition to free Wi-Fi and parking, it provides rooms with a modern, functional design. *82 rooms | Ctra. de Roses Polígon Vilatenim Sud | tel. 972 50 15 87 | www.sidorme.com | Budget*

INFORMATION

OFICINA DE TURISME
Plaça del Sol | tel. 972 50 31 55 | www.figueresciutat.com

WHERE TO GO

PERALADA (120 B4) (*∅ E4*)
This medieval town (pop. 1300) is situated 7km/4mi north-east of Figueres. The 14th century ● castle attracts thousands

of visitors every year because a gaming casino *(daily 8pm–4am)* is housed here. It is also home to the ★ *Museu del Castell de Peralada.* Collections of glass objects, ceramics, books and paintings as well as a historic wine cellar (with wine tasting!) bear witness to the glamour of the Catalan upper classes. *Daily guided tours 10am, 11am and midday, in summer hourly 4pm–8pm | admission 5 euros | www.casino-peralada.com*

TERRA REMOTA BODEGA
(120 B3) *(ᗰ E3)*

Some 13km/8mi north of Figueres, in Sant Climent Sescebes, the Bournazeau family has brought back to life former vineyards and a bodega, a winery, equipped with the very latest technology. White and red wines are produced here. You can visit the bodega and taste the wine, if you order in advance there is a INSIDER TIP picnic basket with ham, cheese and wine. *Mon–Sat 9am–midday and 2pm–6pm | Sant Climent Sescebes, 6km/4mi towards Company | tel. 9 72 19 37 27 | www.terraremota.com*

L'ESCALA

(123 E2) *(ᗰ F6)* **The town has more than 5000 inhabitants, and easily ten times as many in summer.**

Hotels, shops and pubs line the main beach promenade. But the small *norte* district by the port with its bars and cosy restaurants is very different. L'Escala is the home port of around fifty small trawlers, making it, next to Roses, one of the most important fishing ports on the Costa Brava.

SIGHTSEEING

INSIDER TIP **CEMENTERIO DE L'ESCALA**

'Beautiful in its isolation, simple and noble, dressed in white, the colour of peace, beneath a splendid sun and the great blue sky.' This was how the Catalan writer Caterina Albert described this cemetery, where she herself was buried in 1966. *Carrer Garbí, 15 | usually closed, but you can get the key from the town hall*

PUNTA MONTGÓ ⚲
Cala Montgó, a lovely bay with fine sand, is situated approx. 4km/2.5mi to the south but it has unfortunately been rather built up. Above the bay are the ruins of a medieval watchtower with views over the sea.

FOOD & DRINK

EL ROSER 2
This first class restaurant has had a great reputation for many decades for its seafood and homemade desserts. Their specialities are lobster and prawns. *Closed Wed | Passeig Lluis Albert, 1 | tel. 9 72 77 02 19 | Expensive*

ELS PESCADORS
The name says it all, mainly fish and seafood is served here. The restaurant has a fresh, white ambience and you can also sit out on the terrace. It is famous for *zarzuela*, a fish and shellfish stew. *Closed Sun evening and Thu | Cove Port d'en Perris, 5 | tel. 9 72 77 07 28 | Expensive*

LOS COMPADRES
This is a small bar where you can enjoy excellent mussels. *Closed Thu | Carrer Bonaire, 13 | tel. 9 72 77 08 55 | Budget*

SHOPPING

The shops with souvenir items are situated in the southern part of the town, above the fishing port. Market days are Thursdays and Saturdays on *Plaça Victor Catala.* Every Sunday there is also a clothes market on *Passeig del Mar.*

Mending their fish traps: L'Escala is one of the most important fishing ports on the Costa Brava

SPORTS, ACTIVITIES & BEACHES

BEACHES

The nicest bathing bays are to the north. You can walk there on the *Camí Forestal*. Over a stretch of a few miles there is one bay after another. *Cala Montgó*, for example, to the south is very popular with tourists.

WATER SPORTS

On offer at *Funtastic Empordà* there is diving, sailing, surfing and water skiing, and you can also get lessons and hire equipment. *Platja de Riells, s/n | tel. 972 77 41 84 | www.funtastic-emporda.com*

ENTERTAINMENT

The discos and bars are mainly in the south of the town. In the old town, on the other hand, it is rather more sedate, and there is a row of bars frequented by locals and just a few tourists.

WHERE TO STAY

HOTEL CAN MIQUEL

This hotel is situated right on Montgó beach with views of the sea. It has modern, rather sober furnishings, the rooms are a little small but, given the location, it is good value for money. *34 rooms | Platja Montgó | tel. 9 22 77 14 52 | Moderate*

VISTA ALEGRE ❄️

The 'happy view', as this small guesthouse is called, looks out over the sea. It is right on the beach and the staff are friendly. *16 rooms | Carrer El Cargol, 16 | tel. 60 72 02 25 80 | www.vistaalegre.biz | Budget*

VORAMAR

This comfortable hotel is situated on the edge of the old town right on the seaside promenade and some rooms have a sea view. *34 rooms | Passeig Lluis Albert, 2 | tel. 972 77 01 08 | www.hotelvoramar. com | Expensive*

INFORMATION

OFICINA DE TURISME
Plaça Escoles Nacionals, 1 | tel. 972 77 06 03 | www.lescala-empuries.com

WHERE TO GO

EMPÚRIES
(123 E 1–2) *(∅ F6)*

Just inland from the sea, some 2km/1mi north of L'Escala, is a large excavation site which has unearthed traces of human life dating back 6000 years. Finds of coins are evidence that Greeks settled here later, followed by Romans, Goths – and even pirates. Empúries reflects, therefore, the whole history of settlement in this area. The site was restored at the start of the 19th century and opened to visitors. A small museum has exhibits of archaeological finds. *Museu d'Arqueologia Empúries | 1 June–30 Sept daily 10am–8pm, Oct–31 May daily 10am–6pm | admission 3 euros | www.mac.es*

INSIDER TIP SANT MARTI D'EMPÚRIES
(123 E1) *(∅ F6)*

Go for a walk along the coast heading north and, after 3km/2mi, you will come to this medieval village. Fishermen founded a holy site here in the 9th century and a Gothic church was later added. It is worth going to have a look at the old forestry house on a hill on the edge of the village.

LLANÇÀ

(121 D3) *(∅ G3)* **The centre of Llançà was laid out a few miles inland from the** **port for fear of pirates. Today the village (pop. 4000) has been ruinously over-developed, with hardly a gap between the buildings, and the few remaining old squares are rapidly disappearing.**

Tourism and anchovy fishing are the most important factors in the town's economy. Llançà is blessed with an excellent range of small quiet beaches and coves. It is ideal for summer visitors looking for a relatively quiet atmosphere, but at the same time still wanting to be able to enjoy beaches, restaurants and bars.

SIGHTSEEING

EL CAMPANAR

In front of this Romanesque bell tower there is a huge plane tree, the Tree of Liberty. It was planted by Liberals and a local priest prevented Franco's soldiers from felling it in 1939. *Plaça Major*

ESGLÈSIA DE SANT VICENÇ

The fabulous main steps lined with cannon balls are the most striking feature of this Baroque church. *Plaça Major*

FOOD & DRINK

INSIDER TIP ELS PESCADORS ☺

This is a large, bright terrace restaurant overlooking the port. It is run by members of the *La cuina del vent* collective, committed to sustainably grown local produce. Here you can enjoy all manner of seafood and, of course, homemade desserts. *Closed Sun evening and Mon | Carrer Castellar, 41 | tel. 972 38 01 25 | Expensive*

LA BRASA

This small restaurant with terrace specialises in fish, octopus and paella. But you can also get grilled lamb chops here. *Closed Mon evening and Tue | Plaça Catalunya, 6 | tel. 972 38 02 02 | Moderate*

SHOPPING

The market day is Wednesday, when you can pick up *garnatxa,* a speciality sweet wine grown in this area.

SPORTS, ACTIVITIES & BEACHES

SEA KAYAKING

SK-Kayak | Carrer Farella, 25 | tel. 6 27 43 33 32 | www.skkayak.com

SAILING

Seven-day sailing courses for different age groups and abilities are available. The beginner course costs, for example, 160 euros. *Club Nàutic Llança | Port de Llança | tel. 9 72 38 07 10 | www.cnllanca.cat*

BEACHES

The local coast is very rocky and there are ● lots of small bays, most of them without sanitary facilities, kiosk or lifeguard. On the 170m long *Grifeu* beach, some 15.5km/10mi heading towards Portbou, there are showers and toilets, and the beach is cleaned every day.

DIVING

Centre d'Immersió | Carrer Martinez Lozano, 9 | Cap de Creus | tel. 9 72 12 00 00 | www.cicapcreus.com

WHERE TO STAY

HOTEL BERI

Affordable, centrally located hotel with its own car park and swimming pool on the roof that represents good value for money. *60 rooms | La Creu, 17 | tel. 9 72 38 01 98 | www.hotel-beri.com | Budget*

HOTEL GRIFEU

Situated just outside Llança, the hotel is right on Grifeu beach. The box-like hotel with small balconies dates from the 1950s but has since been renovated several times. It is basic and some ☆ rooms have a sea view. *37 rooms | Ctra. de Portbou, s/n | tel. 9 72 38 00 50 | www.hotelgrifeu.com | Moderate*

HOTEL GRIMAR

The hotel surrounded by gardens dates from the beginnings of tourism on the Costa Brava. It has been family-run for three generations, regularly renovated and has a swimming pool and tennis court. The rooms have a balcony with a view of the garden. *45 rooms | Ctra. de Portbou, s/n | tel. 9 72 38 01 67 | www.hotelgrimar.com | Expensive*

INFORMATION

PATRONAT MUNICIPAL DE TURISME

Avenida Europe, 37 | tel. 9 72 38 12 58 | www.lanca.cat

WHERE TO GO

INSIDER TIP **EL PORT DE LA SELVA** ☆ (121 E3) (*Ø G4*)

A 7km/4mi winding country road takes you to El Port de la Selva. The skyline of the village is a good indication that is not dominated by tourism. The white buildings are still constructed to normal house height, and fishing boats rather than yachts bob up and down in the harbour. It is a tranquil place for a stroll by the sea or a swim in the shallow water.

You can enjoy very good fish in the *Ca L'Herminda (daily | Carrer Illa, 7 | tel. 9 72 38 70 75 | Expensive).* But you should book for this restaurant, which is also very popular with locals, if you want to avoid a lengthy wait. The hotel *Porto Cristo (52 rooms | Carrer Major, 59 | tel. 9 72 38 70 62 | www.hotelportocristo.com | Expensive)* is situated in the village centre and has been family-run for decades. The building dates from the 19th century and its furnishings are correspondingly dignified.

SANT PERE DE RODES ⅍
(121 D4) (*ⅉ G4*)

This former monastery is situated around 15km/9mi from Llançà in the heart of the mountains. Early chroniclers mention the Benedictine abbey as early as the 9th century. The monastery was abandoned around 1798 and was for a long time left to the wind and weather. The view from the site, which has now been restored – of

PORTBOU

(121 D2) (*ⅉ G2*) Portbou is where the Costa Brava actually begins, but most holidaymakers only experience the village with 2500 inhabitants as they travel through it.

This is doing the place an injustice, because if you are looking to escape from the hustle and bustle and you value a village atmosphere, then this is a quiet and peaceful place where you can feel very relaxed.

The Benedictine monastery of Sant Pere de Rodes has splendid views of bays and mountains

the sea, bays, mountains and El Port de la Selva in the valley – is impressive, especially at sunset. There is also a small restaurant. *June–Sept Tue–Sun 10am–7pm, Oct–May Tue–Sun 10am–5.30pm | admission 4.50 euros, car park 1.50 euros*

SIGHTSEEING

STATION ●

The impressive building, an iron construction with 14 cantilevered arches, was designed by Gustave Eiffel in 1929. Once train travellers coming from France had to wait because trains had to be changed from standard gauge to Spanish gauge at the border station.

CEMENTERIO MUNICIPAL
The number 563 grave at the town cemetery is that of the German Jewish philosopher Walter Benjamin, who fled from the Nazis and took his own life in Portbou in 1940 rather than be handed over to the Gestapo.

BEACH WALK
From the tourist office heading north a path winds its way around cliffs and bays to the *Platja del Pi*. If you want to carry on walking, you can explore the subsequent caves and bays.

FOOD & DRINK

L'ANCORA ☆
Seafood restaurant furnished as in the olden days, with a terrace outside that has a view of the bay. *Closed Mon evening and Tue | Passeig de la Sardana, 3 | tel. 9 72 39 00 25 | Moderate*

ENTERTAINMENT

Party nights do not exist here. Instead you can go for a lovely walk by the sea or on the small *rambla* or enjoy your evening meal outdoors overlooking the sea.

WHERE TO STAY

COMODORO BED & BREAKFAST
Family hotel that is only open from June to September. The rooms are small and furnished without a great deal of style. Breakfast is homemade. It is a place to stay as you pass through. *14 rooms | Carrer Méndez Núñez, 1 | tel. 6 09 47 15 04 | Budget*

INFORMATION

OFICINA DE TURISME DE PORTBOU
Passeig Lluís Companys, s/n | tel. 9 72 12 51 61 | www.portbou.cat

WHERE TO GO

COLERA (121 D2) (*Ⓜ F–G3*)
South of Portbou (approx. 6km/4mi towards Llançà) is the small village of Colera (pop. 450). Only very few visitors find their way here. Perhaps it is the nearby railway bridge almost spanning the whole village which puts them off. On the other hand, the village has a lovely beach, *Platja Garbet*.

ROSES

(121 D–E5) (*Ⓜ G5*) **The town (pop. 12,000) is located on the wide Roses bay with long white beaches, and there was a Greek settlement here in 400 BC.** Tourism took hold from the middle of the 1960s, permanently changing the place. The wide plain close to the sea provided room for the establishment of a holiday resort attracting millions of holidaymakers every year. Roses can, therefore, provide everything you could want from a beach holiday, but has not been able to preserve its original character.

SIGHTSEEING

CIUTADELLA
The octagonal fortress has a long history. The Greeks built a base here in the 5th century BC and in the following centuries the fortress was constantly extended. The French stationed a large garrison here during the Franco-Spanish War. With a total area of over 12 acres, there was room for military facilities as well as accommodation for men and animals. Today the site

no longer has a military use. But the impressive large open space is worth seeing. *Daily 10am–6pm | admission 3 euros | on Avinguda de Rhode*

MUSEU DE LA CIUTADELLA

The history of the village is displayed here. *June/Sept Tue–Sun 10am–8pm, July/Aug Tue–Sun 10am–9pm, Oct–May Tue–Sun 10am–6pm, Nov–Feb Tue–Sat 10am–6pm, Sun 10am–2pm | admission 3 euros | Avinguda de Rhode, s/n | www.rosesfhn.org*

sample the shrimps caught at Roses, but they do come at a certain price. Otherwise there is *suquet*, a traditional dish comprising fish and potatoes, as well as various meat dishes. *Daily | Gola se L'Estany, 79 | tel. 9 72 15 06 78 | Expensive*

DIE INSEL

The head chef may be German, but this restaurant specialises in Spanish cuisine and fresh local produce. The fish dishes such as *zarzuela* and paella are particu-

The Bay of Roses is lined with mile long stretches of white sandy beach

PUIG ROM ☆

The 225m/738ft high Puig Rom rises up in the east of Roses bay. From the summit you have the best view of the bay and town. A 4km/2.5mi long walk leads from the Ciutadella to the viewing point. In the tourist office *(see p. 49)* you can pick up a leaflet with further walking trails.

ALMADRABA PARK ☆

In the elegant hotel restaurant you can enjoy fantastic sea views and **INSIDER TIP**

larly to be recommended, and they also serve excellent juicy steaks. *Closed Tue | Carrer Pescadors, 17 | tel. 9 72 15 37 57 | www.dieinsel.info/EN | Expensive*

EL JABALÍ ☺

This is a bright restaurant decorated in green and yellow and with a small terrace. Mediterranean cuisine using fresh produce from the local market. *Closed Wed | Cala Rostella, 13 | tel. 9 72 25 65 25 | Moderate*

SI US PLAU ☀

The small ice cream parlour with terrace is situated right on the beach. *Daily | Passeig Maritím, 1 | tel. 9 72 25 42 64 | Budget*

SÓDEMAR

A combination of meat and seafood is served, for example *pies de cerdo rellenos de langostinos* (pig's trotters stuffed with crayfish). *Closed Mon | Port Nautic de Roses | tel. 9 72 15 20 34 | Expensive*

SHOPPING

Shops of interest to tourists are to be found in the streets behind *Plaça Catalunya*. There are two Sunday markets: the clothes market around *Granvia Pau Casalas* as well as a vegetable market *(Carrer Maria Benlliure, s/n)*.

SPORTS, ACTIVITIES & BEACHES

BEACHES

Roses has a mile long beach on its doorstep. There are smaller bathing bays to be found, especially to the east, beyond the fishing port. The small, family-friendly beach *Platja de Canyelles Petites* is particularly nice.

DIVING

The well equipped diving centre provides various diving courses in the vicinity of Roses, and also at Cap de Creus. *Roses Sub Diving Center | Carrer d'Eugeni d'Ors, 15 | tel. 9 72 15 24 26 | www.rosessub.com*

WHERE TO STAY

HOTEL CANYELLES PLATJA

This hotel is situated above the *Canyelles Petites* beach on the Bay of Roses. Some rooms have a sea view. Furnishing suitably modern, though a little spartan. *100 rooms | Av. Díaz Pacheco, 7–9 | tel. 9 72 25 65 00 | www.hotelcanyelles.com | Moderate*

HOTEL CASA DEL MAR

The reasonably priced, well run family hotel (situated in the town but right near the beach) has bright and friendly rooms and a lovely small garden. It is closed from mid October to the end of March. *17 rooms, 11 apartments | Carrer Canigó, 23 | tel. 9 72 25 64 50 | www.hotel-casadelmar.com | Budget*

INSIDER TIP ▶ VISTABELLA ☀

This is arguably the finest and most beautiful hotel on the Bay of Roses. The name provides what it promises: a beautiful view of the sea. In addition, it enjoys a quiet location, immediately behind the lovely beach *Platja de Canyelles Petites*. *30 rooms | Cala Canyelles Petites, s/n | tel. 9 72 25 62 00 | www.vistabellahotel.com | Expensive*

INFORMATION

OFICINA MUNICIPAL DE TURISME

Avinguda de Rhode 72–79 | tel. 9 72 25 73 31 | www.roses.cat

WHERE TO GO

CASTELLÓ D'EMPÚRIES

(120 C5) (*ⓜ F4–5*)

The former residence of the Counts of Empúries is situated 11km/7mi inland (towards Figueres). The noblemen have left behind a palace and thick walls surrounding the small village (pop. 2500) with its narrow streets. The *Basilica de Santa Maria* dating from 1067 with an almost 70m/230ft high tower is well worth a visit. The church was built in early Gothic style on the ruins of a Romanesque church and was restored in the 14th century. The Gothic facade and the INSIDER TIP ▶ columned por-

Empúriabrava: the artificial lagoon town is situated between river landscape and sea

tal with the twelve apostles are particularly worth seeing. *Winter daily 10am–1pm and 3pm–5pm, summer daily 9am–6pm | admission 3 euros | tel. 972 15 62 33 | www.castellodempuries.org | information: Oficina de Turisme | Plaça Jaume, 1*

EMPÚRIABRAVA (120 D5) (*⌀ F5*)

In 1967, after a lengthy debate and much protest from the long-term residents, the site (11km/7mi from Roses) where cows once grazed, gave way to a lagoon town with artificial canals and 2500 mooring points. This holiday resort with more than 24km/15mi of waterways, as well as many tourist facilities has now become a popular resort for long-stay holidaymakers.

PARC NATURAL DELS AIGUAMOLLS DE L'EMPORDÀ ★ ● ☺

(120–121 C–D 5–6) (*⌀ F5*)

The nature reserve extends over one of the largest wetlands in Catalonia, fed by the rivers Muga and Fluvia. The area is a stopping off place for thousands of migratory birds on their way south or north. It is home to amphibians and aquatic animals throughout the year and rare plants survive here. In the park information centre there are leaflets and maps on the surrounding area and the animals to be observed, and you can also hire binoculars. There are two signposted routes through the park with viewing points over the lagoons where ducks and geese splash about and, during the migration periods, whole flocks of up to 100 different species descend. Both routes can be combined with a walk on the nearby beach.

The nature reserve is an unspoilt refuge for animals and plants on and in the water and is the ideal place for those who want to escape the busy beach life for a while. *Admission free | visitors centre with lots of information in Cortalet, some 12km/7.5mi from Roses | daily 9.30am–2pm and 4.30pm–7pm | www.parcsdecatalunya. net*

BAIX EMPORDÀ

Nowhere else on the Costa Brava is the land as varied as here, where culture is so deeply rooted in the history of the Spanish Mediterranean coast.

The Iberians settled in the fertile plains around the Rio Ter in around 800 BC, developing the cradle of the Spanish culture. The land itself is a great garden with cork oaks and pine forests, vineyards, olive groves and corn fields. Inland from the coast there are still oases off the beaten track: small towns and villages with narrow streets and a lifestyle reminiscent of bygone days with weekly markets selling regional produce, proud estates, old churches and country inns with authentic regional cuisine. However, the coast is very popular in summer because this part of the Costa Brava is where the most beautiful bathing bays are to be found.

BEGUR

(123 F5) *(⊞ G9)* **This well-maintained town (pop. 3980) is surrounded by hills covered with pines and is just a stone's throw from coves with crystal clear water.**

The inhabitants have smartened the place up for tourism, but have at the same time managed to preserve its rural character.

Photo: The Bay of Sa Tuna north of Begur

A landscape of many facets: medieval towns, pine forests, beautiful bays and excellent gastronomy

There was a time when the coral trade flourished in this area. After that people lived mainly from the cork industry, but its decline forced many inhabitants to emigrate to South America. Those who returned brought a certain prosperity with them which is still evident today in the *casas de los indianos,* handsome buildings with arcades, in some of the town's streets.

CASTELL DE BEGUR ☆

The hill above the town centre was fortified as far back as the 11th century. A castle was built here in the 15th century, which was later destroyed in the Franco-Spanish War. Little more than ruins now remain, but from here you can enjoy a splendid view of Begur and its surroundings.

Pretty town with a village character: Begur with its castle ruins high above the town centre

ESGLÉSIA SANT PERE

A small Gothic church from the 16th and 17th century, it forms, with the *Plaça d'Església* and *Plaça de la Vila* squares, a picturesque centre with small cosy cafés.

MIRADOR SANT RAMON ☀

Beneath the castle ruins, the *Plaça Sant Ramon* provides a vantage point from with some lovely views of Begur and its bays.

FOOD & DRINK

CAN NASI

Light modern food is served using local produce, as well as fish dishes. Lovely garden. *Sept–May closed Tue, June–Aug daily | Carrer Concepció Pi i Tató, 9 | tel. 9 72 62 21 03 | www.cannasi.com | Budget*

CANCLIMENT

This tastefully decorated restaurant bears the name of the young chef who learned his trade with well-known master chefs. The result is a new ambitious Catalan cuisine: for example, the vegetable dish *huerta de Empordá. Daily | Carrer Onze de Setembre, 27 | tel. 9 72 62 20 31 | Expensive*

INSIDER TIP ▶ ROSTEI ☺

An old wisteria spreads across the terrace of this restaurant in a building dating back to 1849. While the setting may be old, the cuisine is new, with fresh local market produce. The emphasis is on fish dishes, and the desserts are homemade. *Closed Mon | Carrer de Concepció Pi, 8 | tel. 9 72 62 27 04 | www.restaurantrostei.com | Moderate–Expensive*

SHOPPING

On Wednesdays fruit and vegetables and bric-a-brac are sold on *Plaça de la Vila*. There is an arts and crafts market on Thursdays in the summer.

SPORTS & ACTIVITIES

≫ From Begur you can take a 9km/6mi **INSIDER TIP** circular walk to *Aiguafreda* via the *Mirador de la Creu*, which offers an extended view of the coast, and back to Begur. The starting point is the *Masia d'en Pinc* belonging to the flamenco dancer Carmen Amaya in *Passeig de Carmen Amaya*. You can pick up a leaflet about the walk from the tourist office.

ENTERTAINMENT

In addition to a few bars in Begur and the hotel restaurants on the bays, in summer **INSIDER TIP** *carpas* (entertainment tents) are erected, where various performances take place.

WHERE TO STAY

INSIDER TIP AIGUACLARA

The rooms in the 19th century historic building are individually and stylishly furnished, and there is a restaurant, bar, terrace and reading room. *10 rooms | Carrer Sant Miquel, 2 | tel. 9 72 62 29 05 | www.aiguaclara.com | Expensive*

HOTEL ROSA

Located in the town centre, this is an informal hotel with a cosy restaurant. *23 rooms | Calle Pi i Ralló, 11 | tel. 9 72 62 30 15 | info@hotel-rosa.com | Moderate*

INFORMATION

OFICINA MUNICIPAL DE TURISME
Avinguda 11 de Setembre, 5 | tel. 9 72 62 45 20 | www.begur.org

WHERE TO GO

CAP DE BEGUR ★ (123 F5) (𝄞 G9)
The Cape of Begur begins some 4km/2.5mi north of Begur with ● *Aiguafreda* and *Sa Tuna,* magnificent bays framed by rocky cliffs and pine trees. Take a narrow winding road south of Begur and after about

---

MARCO POLO HIGHLIGHTS

5km/3mi you will come to *Fornells*, *Aigua-blava*, *Aiguaxelida* and the largest town of *Tamariu*. These resorts with their lovely bays and delightful small beaches attract numerous visitors in summer.

The outstanding beach is INSIDER TIP *Aiguablava* and the name 'blue water' says it all: nowhere else on the Costa Brava is the sea so magnificently blue, clear and clean as on this bay. In a small pine wood above Aiguablava is the hotel 🌣 *Aiguablava (85 rooms | Platja de Aiguablava | tel. 9 72 62 20 58 | www. aiguablava.com | Expensive)* with an extended view over the coast.

PALS ● 🌣 (123 E4) (*ⵀ G8–9*)

The village of Pals (pop. 1700) is situated 5km/3mi west of Begur. It is a medieval gem full of restored buildings. These include a Romanesque tower, the Romanesque *Sant Pere* church with a Baroque door, as well as fortification walls with four square towers and the village square *Plaça Major.* Beneath Pals there is a long beach with rather coarse sand which is ideal for children because of its gentle slope and clean water, and there is a small beach bar for drinks and snacks. The antennas of the former Radio Liberty tower up into the sky at the end of the beach.

LA BISBAL

(123 D4–5) (*ⵀ E–F9*) ★ **Some 8000 people live in this quiet, rural town on the Rio Daró. It only gets really lively on a Friday when it is market day.**

Most visitors come here in search of beautiful ceramics. Pottery has been produced in Bisbal since the 16th century and, since the 19th century, on an industrial scale. There has been a famous ceramics school here since 1972, teaching design and tech-

nology. In addition to ceramics, agriculture is an important source of income, and the surrounding land is rich in olives, wine and vegetables.

SIGHTSEEING

CARRER DEL CALL

This narrow street is the centre of Bisbal's Jewish quarter and lots of small shops have been set up in the old houses. Take a walk – also through the side streets as they are well worth seeing – and you will experience a sense if its medieval past.

CASTELL PALAU DE LA BISBAL

The bishops of Girona had their seat in Bisbal in the Middle Ages. This Romanesque fortress palace, built in the 11th century and subsequently frequently extended, provided the bishops with additional security by uniquely positioning the chapel on the roof of the defences. A trap door in the chapel leads directly to the Bishop's quarters below. You can visit the bishop's former residence with kitchen, wine cellar, stables and store rooms as well as the palace prison. The historic archive is also housed in the Castell. *Summer Tue–Sat 11am–2pm and 5.30pm–8.30pm, winter Mon–Fri 10am–1pm and 3pm–5pm, Sat 11am–2pm and 5pm–8pm, Sun 11am–2pm | admission 2 euros | Plaça del Castell, s/n*

PONT VELL

The bridge built across the Rio Daró in 1606 is still in use. *Carrer del Pont | south of the large road bridge*

TERRACOTTA MUSEU DE CERÁMICA INDUSTRIAL ●

The ceramics museum, renovated in 2012, provides an overview of the different working methods. *June–Sept Tue–Sat 11am–2pm and 4.30pm–8.30pm | admis-*

sion 3 euros | Calle Sis de Octubre, 99/C/ Industria

FOOD & DRINK

DIVINUM

Located beneath the arcades, this small restaurant serves mainly light modern food using local produce. *Closed Sun| Les Voltes, 19 | tel. 9 72 64 69 77 | Budget*

LA CANTONADA

This is a small but very popular restaurant with an upmarket cuisine. Vegetarian food is also available and the menu changes daily. It is open during the week from 1pm–4pm, at weekends also from 8pm. *Closed Tue | Carrer del Bisbal, 6 | tel. 9 72 64 34 13 | Budget*

SHOPPING

CARRER AIGÜETA

Countless ceramics shops display their wares on this main road to Girona.

INSIDER TIP FRIDAY MARKET

The market is held in the old town and sells produce typical of the area such as olive oil, wine and cold meats. *Fri 8am–2pm | Plaça del Castell*

WHERE TO STAY

HOTEL CASTELL D'EMPORDÀ

Dalí failed in his attempt to purchase the estate in 1973 and it is now a hotel. It is situated a little way outside the town in open countryside in an old castle. This hotel is really something very special with antique furniture, historic walls and extended views of the surrounding countryside, **INSIDER TIP** *especially from the tower room. 14 rooms | Castell d'Empordà, s/n | tel. 9 72 64 62 54 | www.castelldemporda. com | Expensive*

HOTEL MAR DE TASMANIA

The hotel, opened in 2008, is housed in a historic building on the river. It is tastefully furnished in bright colours and has a small

Colourful and rustic: La Bisbal is famous for its wide range of pottery

Showpiece: in Peratallada every stone remains just as it was in the Middle Ages

garden restaurant. *6 rooms | Plaça Francesc Macià, 1 | tel. 9 72 64 05 21 | www.hotel mardetasmania.es | Moderate*

INFORMATION

OFICINA DE TURISMO
Edifici Torre Maria | Carrer Aigüeta, 17 | tel. 9 72 64 55 00 | www.visitlabisbal.cat

WHERE TO GO

CASA-MUSEU CASTELL GALA DALÍ ★
(122 C4) (*M E8*)

Salvador Dalí's castle, where he lived for a long time with his muse Gala, is hidden away in the countryside around Púbol, about 12km/7.5mi north-west of Bisbal. A wealth of memorabilia, such as paintings and drawings, Gala's haute-couture dresses, elephant sculptures in the garden and furniture, give testimony to the life of the famous eccentric. There is even the American road cruiser which Dalí once gave to his adored Gala. *15 March–14 June and 16 Sept–1 Nov Tue–Sun 10am–6pm, 2 Nov–31 Dec Tue–Sun 10am–5pm, 15 June–15 Sept daily 10am–8pm | admission 8 euros | www.salvadordali.org*

INSIDER TIP ▶ CRUÏLLES (123 D5) (*M E9*)

Heading west 4km/2.5mi from Bisbal on the GI 664, you will arrive in Sant Miquel de Cruïlles where there is a collection of well preserved buildings that include a castle, church and monastery ruins, in part dating from the 11th century. The surroundings are ideal for a walk and a picnic.

PERATALLADA ★ (122 D–E4) (*M F8*)

This village (pop. 500, 6km/4mi east of Bisbal) is actually no longer a genuine village anymore; instead it is a place where well-to-do foreigners and people from Barcelona live. Every effort has been made to ensure that each stone remains just as it was in the Middle Ages, creating a showpiece with angular alleys and flowers in the windows, but without crowing cockerels or anything you would associate with genuine village life.

ULLASTRET ★ (123 D4) (*∅ F8*)

9km/6mi north of Bisbal is the excavation site of Ullastret. When the Greeks arrived in the area in the 5th century BC, they found Iberian settlements here, one of them being Ullastret. It is quite clear that there had been a well organised community here: fortifications and storage facilities ensured there was a supply of food even if the harvest was poor. Trade must also have flourished, as is evident from the finds of coins. Today this complex, situated on a hill and surrounded by slender cypresses and gnarled olive trees, feels like a park. A small museum provides information about the origins of Iberian culture. *June–Sept Tue–Sat 10am–8pm, Oct–May daily 10am–2pm and 3pm–6pm | admission 2.30 euros*

PALAMÓS

(125 F2) (*∅ F–G10*) ★ Palamós was a wealthy town as far back as the 16th century. It was sustained by the cork industry and fishing, and the town was once a famous naval base.

Thanks to one of the largest fishing fleets on the Costa Brava, there are still some 13,000 people living here today who make their livelihood from fishing, but since the 1960s they have also been benefiting from tourism. Everything is in place here for holidaymakers: restaurants, hotels and every kind of entertainment. But there is still a hint of an authentic port town. And there are, of course, fine sandy beaches.

SIGHTSEEING

ESGLÉSIA SANTA MARIA

With its square tower and pyramid-like roof, the late Gothic church dominates the town skyline. The altar is decorated with Flemish School paintings. *Plaça de l'Església*

INSIDER TIP ▶ **MUSEU DE LA PESCA**

The fishing museum is the pride and joy of the inhabitants of Palamós. Its focus is the study, preservation and promotion of the Costa Brava's maritime and fishing heritage, and no expense has been spared in mounting a presentation of everything connected with fishing: its history, equipment, catching methods, the social life of the fishermen and anecdotes. The introductory video is available in English. *15 June–15 Sept daily 10am–9pm, 16 Sept–14 June Mon–Sat 10am–1.30pm and 3pm–7pm, Sun 10am–2pm and 4pm–7pm | admission 3 euros | Moll Pesquer | www.museudelapesca.org*

PORT DE PESCA

The return of the fishing boats from sea in the late afternoon provides a **INSIDER TIP** ▶ sight worth seeing repeated day after day, men heaving crates filled with fish on to the quaysides. The catch is taken straight to *La Lotja*, the auction hall, where from 5pm the merchants are seated on a stand and the catch is displayed on a conveyor belt opposite. The merchants do not look directly into the crates of fish, but at a mirror suspended above, enabling them to get a better view of the catch. And then wheeling and dealing begins.

FOOD & DRINK

CELLER DE LA PLANASSA ☺

The food is prepared by the *Cuina de L'Empordanet* cookery collective, using locally grown vegetables. The restaurant is simple and without frills, it has bare stone walls and a pleasant glass-fronted outdoor area and serves mainly fish and rice dishes. *Closed Mon lunch | Carrer del Vapor, 4 | tel. 972 31 64 96 | Expensive*

On Tuesdays you can buy fruit and vegetables direct from the producer at the market in Palamós

CLUB NÀUTIC

Situated right on the port, seafood is of course the speciality. *Daily from 1pm | Zona Port, s/n | tel. 9 72 31 40 48 | Budget*

EL MIRADOR ⬥

Fish and seafood are served at this inn flooded with light on the town outskirts, with a view of the Bay of Palamós. *Closed Tue, Wed and Nov | Plaça de La Murada, 5 | tel. 9 72 31 53 76 | Moderate*

LA GAMBA

This fish restaurant is especially popular with Spanish tourists because of its authentic Mediterranean cuisine. It has a terrace. *Closed Wed and in winter Sun evening | Plaça de Sant Pere, 1 | tel. 9 72 31 46 33 | Moderate*

MARIA DE CADAQUÉS

The restaurant has been family-run for four generations since 1936. The walls are decorated with pictures by local artists, and the tables are rather close together.

Fish dominates the menu, including *suquet,* the traditional fish and potato stew. *Closed Sun evening and Mon | Tauler i Servía, 6 | tel. 9 72 31 40 09 | www.maria decadques.cat | Expensive*

SHOPPING

Most shops are located in *Carrer Major* where you can buy local produce, fresh fruit and wine.

CASA MORERA

This is an old bodega with a great range of spirits and also wine on tap. *Carrer Nou, 8*

SPORTS, ACTIVITIES & BEACHES

SAILING

The ● *Rafael* is a restored boat with lateen sails. It was built in 1915 as a fishing boat and used to sail along the coast. Today you can go on an excursion on the traditional boat and sailing experience is not necessary, though active participation is appreciated. Wind-proof clothing is recommended. *3.5 hours, 27 euros | Tela Marinera | tel. mobile 6 09 30 76 23 | www.telamarinera.es*

BEACHES

There are more than a dozen beaches and bathing bays close to the town of Palamós. The surrounding streets provide the town beach, *Platja Gran* next to the port, with a full range of facilities. The beaches further east beyond the port are quieter, for example *Platja de la Fosca.*

ENTERTAINMENT

There are some bars in the old town and by the port – and that is about it as far as nightlife is concerned. The neighbouring Platja d'Aro has much more to offer *(see p. 62)* in the evenings.

INSIDER TIP CAN MONI

This is a small traditional pub, with all sorts of curiosities hanging on the walls. They serve wine, sparkling wine and above all *montaditos,* skewered delicacies on bruschetta. *Closed Mon | Carrer Mauri i Vilar*

WHERE TO STAY

HOSTAL RESIDENCIA CATALINA

Located in a quiet area, with the port a short walk away, it is clean and the breakfast is substantial. *22 rooms | Carrer Fomento, 16 | tel. 9 72 31 43 86 | www.hostalcatalina.com | Budget*

HOTEL MARINA

A city hotel close to the port, the rooms are relatively small, but the central location is good and they have a garage, which can be an advantage because there is only limited parking in the town. *65 rooms |* *Avinguda Onze de Setembre, 48 | tel. 9 72 60 18 19 | www.hotelmarina-palamos.com | Moderate*

HOTEL SANT JOAN

Housed in an 18th century Catalan farmhouse, with a large garden and swimming pool. It is less than a mile from the beach and the rooms are quite small, but comfortable and nicely furnished, some with sofas. *22 rooms | Avinguda de la Libertad, 79 | tel. 9 72 31 42 08 | Expensive*

HOTEL TRIAS

Situated on the seafront with a view of the Bay of Palamós. The rooms are bright and large, and there is a swimming pool in the courtyard. *81 rooms | Passeig del Mar, s/n | tel. 9 72 60 18 00 | www.hoteltrias.com | Expensive*

INFORMATION

OFICINA DE TURISMO
Carrer Pere Joan, 44 | tel. 9 72 60 05 00 | www.palamos.org

LOW BUDGET

▶ If you use the bus to get about, you can save money by buying a day or multi-day ticket. With the bus company *SARFA*, a single ticket for 1 zone is 2 euros, a ticket for 10 trips just 9.25 euros. Tickets are available at the bus stations.

▶ In the *Museu Municipal* you can get a free overview of the archaeology and history of the region around Sant Feliu de Guíxols. *Tue–Sat 10am–1pm and 5pm–8pm, Sun 10am–1pm | Plaça Monestir | Sant Feliu de Guíxols*

For sun worshippers: Calella de Palafrugell has lovely bays for sunbathing and swimming

WHERE TO GO

CALELLA DE PALAFRUGELL
(123 F6) (*∅ G10*)

This place (11km/7mi north of Palamós) has escaped all the tourist hustle and bustle. Sun worshippers lie between fishing boats on the beach lined with arcades, and houses built right on the beach also contribute to the idyllic scene. Calella de Palafrugell is known for its *habaneras*. You can sometimes hear these melancholic songs of Catalan emigrants at close quarters and in an authentic setting at *La Bella Loca*, a bar on the *Plaça St. Pere, 4.*

The ☀ *Jardines de Cap Roig* are situated in the immediate vicinity of Calella de Palafrugell, to the south. The botanical gardens cover 5.5 acres and were laid out in the 1920s by a Russian ex-officer. The varied landscape garden is home to more than 1200 different Mediterranean plants. You can stroll between cacti, geraniums and ancient tress and enjoy the beneficial peace and quiet and the wonderful views

of the sea. *April–Sept 10am–8pm, Oct–March 10am–6pm | admission 6 euros*

DOLMEN DE LA COVA D'EN DAINA
(125 D2) (*∅ E10*)

This megalithic tomb dating from about 2000 BC was discovered by the road just outside the village of Romanyà de la Selva in 1894. The burial site comprises 36 standing stones which lead down into a circular tumulus with a diameter of 11m/36ft. *About 18km/11mi to the west*

PALAFRUGELL (123 E5) (*∅ G9*)

The vibrant town 8km/5mi north of Palamós was for hundreds of years the centre of the cork industry, but today there are just a few businesses which still process this raw material. The busy *tourist office*, the *Sant Martí* church and a few restaurants are to be found in the centre. On the Plaça Nova there is the attractive *Centre Fraternal*, the INSIDER TIP Palafrugell casino built in 1887 where you can relax over a cup of coffee in its spacious rooms.

There are two museums which are worth visiting. Firstly, the *Fundació Josep Plà* – in the house where the Catalan author Josep Plà was born – contains a collection of his works and lots of his personal belongings. *(16 Sept–14 June Tue–Fri 5pm–8pm, Sat 9.30am–1pm and 5pm–8pm, Sun 10am–1pm, 15 June–15 Sept Tue–Sat 10am–1pm and 5pm–8.30pm, Sun 10am–1pm | admission 2.50 euros, with cork museum 4 euros | Carrer Nou, 49 | www.fundacioseppla.net)*. Secondly, the ● *Museu del Suro* which details everything about cork: the industrial use of the natural product from bottle closure to insulating material and its significance for the region. *(15 June–15 Sept Tue–Sat 10am–1.30pm and 5pm–8.30pm, Sun 10am–1.30pm, 16 Sept–14 June Tue–Sat 5pm–8pm, Sun 10.30am–1.30pm | admission 3 euros | Carrer Tarongeta, 31 | www.museudelsuro.org)*

The INSIDER TIP *Hotel Mas Ses Vinyes (25 rooms | Carretera GIP 6531 direction Begur 1.2km | tel. 9 72 30 15 70 | www.masses vinyes.com | Expensive)* is in a renovated farmhouse amidst open countryside, surrounded by cypresses and pine trees. It provides every comfort such as open fire, jacuzzi, sauna – and large beds. Information: *Entrada de Palafrugell | Carrer del Carrilet, 2 | tel. 9 72 30 02 28 | www.palafrugell.cat*

INSIDER TIP PLATJA DEL CASTELL

(125 F2) (*ⓜ G10*)
This wonderful rocky bay with fine sand and crystal clear water is situated north of Palamós, 2.5km/1.5mi from the main road.

PLATJA D'ARO

(125 E3) (*ⓜ F11*) **Just a few decades ago there was nothing here but gardens, whereas today the beach is lined with large hotel buildings, and numerous fast food restaurants, supermarkets and bars make the place a major tourist centre.**

For holidaymakers wanting to unwind, Platja d'Aro is the ideal base. The beaches are well cared for with fine sand, and in the evenings there are lots of opportunities for entertainment: going for a stroll or out for a meal, having a cocktail or a night out in the disco.

Platja d'Aro is particularly popular with tourists from northern and east European countries. Pleasure craft skippers also appreciate the large port with more than 400 mooring points. In the winter, on the other hand, when most establishments have closed, the 5000 inhabitants are mainly left to themselves.

FOOD & DRINK

ARADI

A traditional restaurant that has been family-owned for 40 years. Fish and lamb dishes are served. *Daily | Avinguda del Cavall Bernat, 78 | tel. 9 72 81 73 76 | Moderate*

EL CAU DE PERNIL

This rustic restaurant will delight meat eaters: there are various sorts of ham and sausage as well as every variety of grilled meat. *Daily | Avinguda Sant Feliu, 7 | tel. 9 72 81 72 09 | Budget*

LA CALA ⚜

Located in the Hotel Silken Park San Jorge, serving traditional local food, including fish dishes. It is nice to sit on the terrace in the shade of the pine trees with a view of the sea. *Daily | Ctra. de Palamós, s/n | tel. 9 72 65 23 11 | Moderate*

SHOPPING

From sun cream to Rolex watches, you can buy anything and everything in hundreds of shops between the streets *Avinguda S'Agaró* and *Passeig Marítim*.

SPORTS, ACTIVITIES & BEACHES

All the fun of the seaside is to be found on the mile long ● *Platja Gran* main beach. The beach – with showers, lifeguards and first aid posts, bars, children's playgrounds, toilets and sports fields – is situated right next to the town. It is a bit calmer in the smaller *Cala Sa Conca* bay south of the town.

But this too has showers, toilets, children's playgrounds and a kiosk bar. At the northern end of Platja d'Aro is *Cala Rovira* bay, more than 200m/650ft long, which also has a complete range of facilities. These sandy beaches have quite coarse sand. And there are also smaller rocky beach coves without any facilities, such as *Cala del Pi* north of the town and *Cala Pedrosa* to the south.

TENNIS

The Club de Tenis d'Aro has 14 sand courts. *Paratge La Gramoia | tel. 9 72 81 74 00*

WATER SPORT

Windsurfing and sailing school as well as board hire at *Escola Municipal de Vela | tel. 9 72 82 57 82*

ENTERTAINMENT

Countless discos, bars, clubs and pubs are open right through the night on *Passeig Marítim* and in the streets behind. There are four discos in *Avinguda S'Agaró* where you can dance: *Costa Azul (no. 120)*, *Malibu (no. 75)*, *Marius (no. 86)* and *Pacha (no. 179)*.

WHERE TO STAY

COSTA BRAVA ⚜

A hotel with an impressive location, built on a cliff directly overlooking the sea with

Tourist centre Platja d'Aro: tall hotel buildings line the fine sandy beach

access to the beach below. Most rooms have a balcony and are relatively large and bright. *60 rooms | Punta d'en Ramis, s/n | tel. 9 72 81 70 70 | www.hotelcosta brava.com | Moderate*

HOSTAL DE LA GAVINA ✳

Luxury hotel on the Bay of S'Agaro offering historic Spanish style rooms, with a view of the sea and also a heated swimming pool, spa and beauty treatments and four restaurants, including *Candlelight* with haute cuisine on the patio. *57 rooms and 17 suites | Plaça Rosaleda, s/n | tel. 9 72 32 11 00 | www.lagavina.com | Expensive*

PANAMÁ

Situated away from the tourist hustle and bustle and relatively quiet. But it is still only 300m/900ft to the beach. The rooms are comfortable, though a little small. *42 rooms | Avinguda S'Agaró, 132 | tel. 9 72 81 76 39 | www.hotelpanama.com | Moderate*

PLANAMAR

This is a four-storey building by the beach. On the top floor there is a swimming pool and restaurant. The rooms are bright and cheerful, ✳ some with sea views. *84 rooms | Passeig del Mar, 82 | tel. 9 72 81 71 77 | www.planamar.com | Budget*

INFORMATION

OFICINA DE TURISME
Carrer M. J. Verdaguer, 4 | tel. 9 72 81 71 79 | www.platjadaro.com

WHERE TO GO

CASTELL D'ARO (125 E3) (⊞ E11)

The small medieval village with the late Gothic church *Santa Maria de Castell d'Aro* is situated 3km/2mi west of Platja d'Aro. The *Castell Benedormiens,* newly erected on the foundations of an old castle, some-

times has temporary art exhibitions. Information: *tel. 9 72 81 72 84* and *cultura@platjadaro.com* ● At the tourist information in Platja d'Aro *(see left)* you can book free guided tours of the village and the *Museu de la Niña* doll museum *(Tue–Fri 6pm–9pm, Sat and Sun 11am–1pm and 6pm–9pm | admission free | Plaça Lluis Companys, s/n)* where you can see more than 800 dolls from various eras.

SANTA MARIA DE SOLIUS MONASTERY (125 D3) (⊞ E11)

The Cistercian monastery, part of which is open to the public, was founded after the Second Vatican Council in 1967. According to the rules of the order, founded in 1098, work and prayer are at the heart of monastic life. The monks come from Poblet Monastery south of Barcelona and have established a refuge for themselves here. The monastery has six modest rooms which are available to men free of charge but a donation is expected. Meals are taken at fixed times with the monks and guests are expected to take part at least once a day in the monks' services. The monastery is, therefore, in no way to be regarded as a place where you can get free holiday accommodation. *Santa Maria de Solius | approx. 11km/7mi on the C 65 towards Llagostera | tel. 9 72 83 70 84 (10am–12.30pm and 3.30pm–5pm)*

SANT FELIU DE GUÍXOLS

▓▓ MAP ON PAGE 127
(125 E3) (⊞ E–F11) ★ **The town with around 15,000 inhabitants is rich in history and has been able, despite tourism, to preserve its style.**
The Iberians were here first and then later the Romans arrived. A major settlement

was established around the Sant Benet Monastery from the 10th century, and a large port with wharves was built in the 12th century. The 18th and 19th centuries were then dominated by the cork industry.

INSIDER TIP CASINO DEL NOIS
Built in 1889, the casino is exquisitely furnished and is a place for relaxation, and it is not only the local senior citizens who do so here. *Passeig dels Guíxols*

Casino del Nois: a beautiful place to relax

The bourgeoisie discovered the restorative properties of the area and built stately villas befitting their elevated status. Today lots of Spanish families also spend their holidays in Sant Feliu as well as visitors simply looking for peace and quiet.

SIGHTSEEING

CASA PATXOT
The ornate villa in the *modernismo* style once belonged to a cork industrialist. Today the impressive building is home to the Chamber of Industry and Commerce. You can admire the interior when exhibitions are held, though these are not all that frequent. *Passeig del Mar, 40*

ERMITA DE SANT ELM
Dedicated to St Elmo, the hermitage sits on a cliff above Cala Vigatà, commanding a fantastic view.

PORTA FERRADA
The restored part of a 10th century portico belonged to the adjacent Benedictine *Sant Feliu* monastery. *Plaça Monestir*

FOOD & DRINK

CAN SALVI
This restaurant, specialising in fish and rice dishes such as paella, has been here since 1949. It is situated right on the seafront promenade and has a maritime ambience

and a terrace. *Closed Thu and Sun evening | Passeig del Mar, 23 | tel. 9 72 32 10 13 | www. restaurantcansalvi.com | Moderate*

CASA BUXÓ

The wood-panelled walls, ceiling beams and clear table arrangement give this restaurant a very comfortable feel. The cuisine is traditional local dishes, fish and meat. *Closed evenings except Fri and Sat | C/ Mayor, 18 | tel. 9 72 32 01 87 | Budget*

EL DORADO MAR ☠

A large restaurant on Rambla Vidal, the street where the people love to stroll, serving fish and meat dishes. *Daily | Passeig Irla, 15 | tel. 9 72 32 62 86 | Expensive*

INSIDER TIP L'AROMA

Nice little breakfast café with cakes, fruit juices and a great selection of teas. *Daily | Plaça del Mercat, 8 | tel. 9 72 32 06 57 | Budget*

SHOPPING

As everywhere else on the Costa Brava, the shops in the streets around *Passeig del Mar* in St Feliu are also very much targeted at tourists. However, here you will find fewer cheap shops than elsewhere, and in the old town there is much better quality. A weekly market is held outside the town hall on Sundays.

SPORTS, ACTIVITIES & BEACHES

SAILING

Take a day trip on the ketch sailboat the *Costa Magica, with a* maximum of 10 passengers plus skipper. For 2 people it will cost about 350 euros. *Escullera del Moll | Pantalà Amarratge, 04 | tel. 9 72 32 33 07 | tel. mobile 6 29 96 08 22 | www.costa magica.net*

BEACHES AND BAYS

There are about a dozen beaches close to the town, and they are quite different. There are those with fine sand, others with coarse sand; some are long, others are in narrow rocky bays. You can pick up an accurate map of the beaches at the tourist office *(see p. 66)*. The *Platja de Sant Pol*, the half mile long town beach has fine sand and a complete range of facilities. In a rocky bay north of the town, only accessible on foot and lined by pine trees, is ● *Cala Amettler*, 300m/900ft long, but there are no sanitary facilities and the sand is coarse.

DIVING

Diving trips and courses are available at *Piscis Diving | Avinguda El Fortim, 97 | tel. 9 72 32 69 58, tel. mobile 6 17 88 54 54 | www.piscisdiving.com*

TENNIS

The *Club Tenis Guíxols* also offers lessons. *Carretera Sant Pol, s/n | tel. 9 72 32 10 50*

ENTERTAINMENT

The old town beyond Passeig del Mar with its bars and discos is where night owls head for. In the evening some bars put on *cançons de taverna,* singing in the style of the Habaneras, songs of a Cuban origin. But things are a lot quieter here than in the neighbouring Platja d'Aro.

WHERE TO STAY

HOSTAL EL CISNE

This basic guesthouse is located in the centre of the town and just a few minutes from the beach. The rooms are bright, but relatively small and rather modestly furnished but, given the location and the standard, it is good value for money. *21* rooms | *Rambla Generalitat, 11 | tel. 9 72 32 48 10 | Budget*

HOTEL S'AGARO MAR ☼

A family hotel, it offers a children's play area and plenty of room in the grounds. It is above the Bay of Sant Pol and offers extensive views. The rooms are bright and cheerful, many with a balcony; there is also a swimming pool. *75 rooms | Cami de la Caleta, 5 | tel. 9 72 32 11 40 | www.ghthotels.com | Expensive*

HOTEL SANT POL

The hotel is right on Sant Pol beach. The colourful rooms are tastefully decorated – ☼ many with sea views, some with jacuzzi – and rather small given the position of the beds. But two great advantages: the lovely location by the sea and the restaurant with daily specials *(Budget)*. *22 rooms | Platja de Sant Pol, 125 | tel. 9 72 32 10 70 | info@hotelsantpol.com | Expensive*

INFORMATION

OFICINA MUNICIPAL DE TURISME
Plaça del Mercat, 28 | tel. 9 72 82 00 51 | www.guixols.net

WHERE TO GO

SANTA CRISTINA D'ARO
(125 D–E3) *(𝄞 E10–11)*

At the time of the cork boom, from 1892, there was a narrow gauge railway which ran through the town transporting the harvested cork. All that now remains of it is the small restored station in which the *restaurant Font Picant (closed Sun | Sta. Cristina d'Àro | Urbanisación Bell-Loc, 1 | tel.9 72 83 33 50 | Moderate)* not only offers outstanding food, for example Argentinian grilled steak, but **INSIDER TIP** Fri and Sat also live jazz music. *5km/3mi west of Sant Feliu*

TORROELLA DE MONTGRÍ

(123 E3) *(𝄞 F7–8)* **This historic town by the banks of the Riu Ter is mentioned in documents as far back as the 9th century.**

Today Torroella de Montgrí (pop. 5600) is well-known for its *sardanas,* the old Catalan circle dances. But it offers the atmosphere of an authentic Spanish town with great cultural diversity. It is true the beach is 6km/4mi away, but here you can leave behind all the hustle and bustle of the tourist trade in the nearby L'Estartit and enjoy peace and quiet. There is a particularly nice walk from *Plaça de la Vila* along *Carrer de L'Església* to the impressive *Sant Genís* church and on to the *Portal Santa Caterina.* Torroella de Montgrí became a royal city at the end of the 13th century and some stately buildings were erected.

SIGHTSEEING

CAN QUINTANA ★ ●

As far as Mediterranean culture is concerned, the Mediterranean Cultural Centre, opened in 2003, is the most interesting museum on the whole of the Costa Brava. The exhibition covers a broad cultural spectrum in the Mediterranean, from Egypt to Tunisia, and Greece to France and Spain. In addition to photos, films, video shows and information panels, the multimedia centre also displays musical instruments and examples of local arts and craft traditions, such as woven baskets and pottery. The museum is particularly interesting for children. *July–Aug Mon–Sat 10am–2pm and 6pm–9pm, Sun 10am–2pm, Sept–June Mon–Sat 10am–2pm and 5pm–8pm, Sun 10am–2pm | admission*

Torroella de Montgrí: a historic town rich with great cultural diversity

free | Carrer d'Ullà, 31 | www.museudela mediterrania.org

CASA DE LA VILA
The arcade-lined town hall dates from the 16th century, and next to it there is the small *Sant Antoni* chapel. *Mon–Sat 11am–2pm and 5pm–8pm*

ESGLÉSIA DE SANT GENÍS
This imposing Gothic church dates from the 14th century *Passeig de L'Església*

PALACIO SOLTERA
The art gallery is housed in this stately Renaissance palace where you can see permanent and also temporary exhibitions, mainly of contemporary Catalan artists. *15 June–15 Sept Tue–Sun 5pm–9.30pm, 16 Sept–14 June Sat 11am–2pm and 4.30pm–8.30pm, Sun 11am–2.30pm | admission 4.50 euros | Carrer de l'Església, 10*

PORTAL SANTA CATERINA
The town gate is beneath one of the well-preserved watchtowers in the 14th cen-tury ramparts. *Behind Sant Genís church on Avinguda De Lluis Companys*

FOOD & DRINK

CAN CARCAN
This restaurant is popular with locals and serves regional food, such as *patatas de olot* (potatoes filled with meat). *Closed Mon | Plaça Ernest Lluch, 61 | tel. 9 72 75 72 99 | Budget*

INSIDER TIP ▶ MOLI DEL MIG ❄
Situated in park-like grounds, in a charmingly resorted old mill building with contemporary designer furnishings and a terrace with wonderful views of the countryside. All the food is prepared using local produce and there is fish, such as *rape* (monkfish), and various meat dishes such as *mar y montaña de pies de cerdo con setas* (pig's trotters with mushrooms and lobster). It is all of the very best quality and prices are surprisingly reasonable. *Camí Molí del Mig, s/n | tel. 9 72 75 53 96 | Budget*

FOOD & DRINK & WHERE TO STAY

MITJÀ

The most reasonably priced accommodation in the town is part of the Mitjà restaurant. The small, pleasant rustic rooms have fieldstone walls. *22 rooms | Carrer Església, 14 | tel. 9 72 75 80 03 | www.fondamitja. com | Budget*

INSIDER TIP PALAU LO MIRADOR

This fine hotel is housed in a former 14th century royal palace. Each suite is named after one of the grandees who once resided here and the furniture dates from the same period. Splendour and luxury, however, come at a price, which also applies to the exquisite restaurant serving imaginative creations of classical regional cuisine and with excellent service. *21 rooms | Passeig de l'Església, 1 | tel. 9 72 75 80 63 | www.palaulomirador.com | Expensive*

SHOPPING

The main shopping streets converge on *Plaça de Vila*. You will struggle to find tourist items in the many small shops. But you can buy the finest pralines at the traditional confectioners *Batlle (Carrer d'Ullà 6)*. The weekly fruit and vegetable market is on Mondays.

ENTERTAINMENT

There is nothing in this small town to disturb the evening peace and quiet except for a few bars and the cinema. If you are looking for entertainment, you should head for L'Estartit a few miles away.

INFORMATION

OFICINA DE TURISME
Passeig Marítim, s/n | L'Estartit | tel. 9 72 75 19 10 | www.visitestartit.com

BOOKS & FILMS

▶ **The Time of the Doves** – the classic of Catalan literature: Mercè Rodoreda tells the life story of a woman whose husband is killed in the civil war and who then has to take responsibility for her own life

▶ **Catalonia A Cultural History** – Michael Eaude traces the area's turbulent history, relates the stories of some of Catalonia's great figures and focuses on Antonio Gaudi's Art Nouveau buildings, exploring the region's artistic legacy

▶ **Little Ashes** – a 2008 Spanish-British film set in 1920s Spain; it follows Salvador Dalí's fortunes as he arrives as a young student in Madrid, meeting Luis Bunuel and Frederica Garcia Lorca

▶ **Vicky Cristina Barcelona** – a romantic Woody Allen comedy (2008) with a star cast (Scarlett Johansson, Javier Bardem and Penelope Cruz): two American girl friends fall in love with a married Spaniard

▶ **Catalan Cuisine** – Colman Andrews explores a once undiscovered gem among Europe's great culinary traditions, using many of the same popular ingredients found in other Mediterranean cuisines, but combining them in fresh and unexpectedly delicious ways

Divers' paradise: the nature reserve islands of Illes Medes off l'Estartit

WHERE TO GO

CASTELL DE MONTGRÍ
(123 E3) (*ⓜ F7*)

This impressive square castle sits majestically on a hill some 300m/900ft high between Torroella and L'Estartit. It was built by King Jaume II from tax revenues from the peasants of Ullà as a symbol of his power in opposition to the Dukes of Empúries. The ascent is arduous and takes about an hour, but the reward is the beautiful panoramic view.

L'ESTARTIT
(123 F3) (*ⓜ G7*)

Today the former fishing village, 6km/4mi from Torroella, is a sprawling tourist centre with lots of hotels, apartments, restaurants and other facilities to cater for the large summer influx. The beach appears endless and flat as far as the northern part, the INSIDER TIP *costa de la mort* (coast of death) as it is called, because this is where many a ship found a watery grave on the rugged rocks.

Water sports are very popular in L'Estartit. For divers in particular it is a great area because of the protected small islands, the *Illes Medes*, lying off the coast. There are numerous diving schools where you can hire equipment, such as *Calypso (open all year | Carrer de La Cala Pedrosa, 1 | tel. 6 09 30 22 01 | www.grn.es/calypso)* or *El Rei del Mar (open all year | Avinguda de Grècia, 5 | tel. 9 72 75 13 92 | www.elrei delmar.com)*. Courses and equipment hire for divers, sailors, kayakers, golfers and water skiers are provided by *Estació Nàutica (Carrer de La Platja | tel. 9 72 75 06 99 | www.enestartit.com)*.

The *Hotel Les Illes (126 rooms | Carrer Les Illes, 55 | tel. 9 72 75 12 39 | www.hotelles illes.com | Budget)* close to the port is where lots of divers stay since the hotel rents out diving equipment and runs courses. The family-friendly *Flamingo (194 rooms | Carrer Església, 112 | tel. 9 72 75 09 27 | info@hotelflamingo.info | Budget) is also a popular hotel*, situated some 300m from the beach.

You can enjoy fish and traditional regional food at the restaurant *La Gaviota (closed in winter | Passeig Marítim, 92 | tel. 9 72 75 20 19 | Budget)*. There are several discos and bars, especially in the area around the port, where you can round off the evening in L'Estartit.

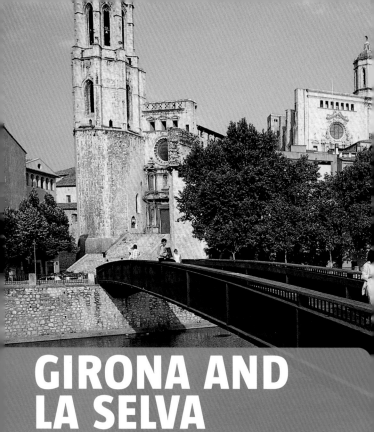

GIRONA AND LA SELVA

Thousands of tourists associate the 'true' Costa Brava with the southernmost part of the Costa Brava.

In summer buses arrive here from all over Europe, full of young people eager for some sun and fun or those looking for an inexpensive holiday. If you don't like crowds and loud, intrusive entertainment, you should avoid the area in the summer. The tide of visitors ebbs perceptibly in the autumn. Empty beaches on which you can stroll for hours, car parking spaces all over the place, discounts everywhere: many Spanish pensioners take advantage of this. In the interior, separated from the coast by wooded mountains, you will find lots of lovely quiet places throughout the year. Just a few miles inland, in a green, hilly landscape, you will come across old villages and hot springs. And you also should not miss out on a visit to Girona, the capital of the province of the same name.

BLANES

(124 B5–6) (ℳ C12–13) **Blanes (pop. 20,000), founded by the Romans, is the terminus of the local train service from Barcelona.**

This is where, heading north, the Costa Brava actually begins. Blanes is a lively

Photo: Girona

Coast of contrasts: lots of fun on the beach and cultural discoveries in the attractive capital of the Costa Brava

town with an important fishing port. The tourist area extends along a mile long bay. The beaches also make Blanes a popular destination for locals from the surrounding area, from as far afield as Barcelona.

SIGHTSEEING

JARDÍ BOTÀNIC MARIMURTRA ★ ⚘
The German scientist Karl Faust (1874–1952) created a beautiful botanical garden on his property. Various gardens with typical Mediterranean plants such as palms and cacti are laid out over an area of 40 acres, and from it you can enjoy a lovely view of Blanes and the sea. *April to Oct daily 9am–6pm, Nov–March daily 9am–8pm | admission 6 euros | Passeig Karl Faust 9 (above the port) | www.jbotanic marimurtra.cat*

With a wonderful location on the coast: the botanical garden Jardí Botànic Marimurtra

FOOD & DRINK

In the fishing port there are some restaurants which are particularly popular with weekend visitors from Barcelona.

CASA OLIVERAS

This is a cosy café with good cakes, coffee and various types of tea. *Daily | Passeig de Dintre, 10 | tel. 9 72 35 75 11 | Budget*

INSIDER TIP ▶ MARISQUERIA EL PORT

Everything the sea offers is served, and the sardines and the *mejillones* (blue mussels) are particularly good. Open from 5am! *Daily | Explanada del Port, s/n | tel. 9 72 33 48 19 | Budget–Moderate*

S'AUGUER

Bright walls and the dark beamed ceiling create a pleasant atmosphere. Fish and seasonal produce dominate the menu. *Closed Wed | Carrer de S'Auguer, 2 | tel. 9 72 35 14 05 | Moderate*

BEACHES

The town beach *Playa Blanes* is more than 600m/1965ft long and starts next to the fishing port. There is fine sand and the full range of facilities, but it is also very busy indeed. The small *Santa Ana* beach with cliffs and coarse sand is situated immediately beyond the port, and showers are available.

Sant Francesc is the name of the bay, lined with pine trees and 200m/650ft long, with fine sand, showers and kiosks about a mile from the centre.

WHERE TO STAY

HOTEL BEVERLY PARK

The hotel occupies a fine position in a tranquil area, just a short stroll away from the resort's longest sandy beach, and it has a fitness room and air conditioning. *168 rooms | Mercè Rodoreda, s/n | tel. 9 72 35 24 26 | www.hotelbeverlypark.com | Moderate*

HOTEL BLAUCEL

Only a pine wood separates the hotel from the beach. It has pools, spa and fitness facilities, and some bedrooms have sea views. *183 rooms | Av. Villa de Madrid, 31 | tel. 9 72 35 85 50 | www.blauhotels blanes.com/en/3/ | Expensive*

PENSIÓ ISABEL

This is a basic guesthouse in the town, about 5 minutes' walk from the beach. It is also not far from the bus station, shops and restaurants. They have family rooms with up to five beds. *37 rooms | C/Josep Tarradellas, 56 | tel. 9 72 33 01 28 | www. hostalisabel.es | Budget*

INFORMATION

OFICINA MUNICIPAL DE TURISME
Plaça Catalunya, 2 | tel. 9 72 33 03 48 | www.blanes.cat

GIRONA

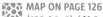 **MAP ON PAGE 126**
(122 A4–5) (*C–D 8–9*) ⭐ In stark contrast to the small coastal towns, the capital of the province of Girona has around 90,000 inhabitants.

It is not only a typical Catalan, but also an ancient Spanish town. The Roman Via Augusta passed through it, the Visigoths settled here in the 6th century, and the town had a large Jewish community in around 900 BC. Felipe III tried to conquer Girona in the Middle Ages, as did the French in 1710, and Franco's troops took the town in February 1939. Girona developed into an important centre for the paper industry in the second half of the 20th century. Go for a walk through the town centre to experience just how attractive Girona is.

SIGHTSEEING

OLD TOWN

The old town lies to the east of Riu Onyar: with narrow streets, lots of steps and parts of the old town walls. The buildings have been renovated and freshly painted, creating a colourful backdrop against the river.

> 🏙 **WHERE TO START?**
> Between **Rambla de Llibertad**, by the Riu Onyar with its colourful house facades, and Carrer Ferreries Velles is Gerona's picturesque *casco antigua*, the heart of the old town with Plaça del Vi, cafés, ancient shops next to ultramodern outlets and the tourist office. It is just a stone's throw from the railway station and there is also parking.

BANYS ARABS

The Moors built these Romanesque public baths (modelled on those in their North African homeland) in the 13th century. *April–Sept Mon–Sat 10am–7pm, Oct–March daily 10am–2pm | admission 2 euros | Carrer Rei Ferran el Catòlic, s/n | www.banysarabs.org*

CARRER DELS ALEMANYS

The 'street of the Germans' is situated beyond *Plaça de Sant Domènec*. In the

---

MARCO POLO HIGHLIGHTS

⭐ **Jardí Botànic Marimurtra**
The Mediterranean rich floral diversity is to be seen in the botanical garden in Blanes → p. 71

⭐ **Girona**
A treasure trove for culture vultures → p. 73

⭐ **Lloret de Mar**
Love it or hate it: the major tourist resort on the Costa Brava → p. 76

⭐ **Tossa de Mar**
Picturesque town in a beautiful location with a medieval ambience → p. 79

17th century this is where a barracks for German mercenaries was built, they had been recruited as a source of protection against the French.

JEWISH QUARTER

In the area around *Carrer de la Força* there are some buildings dating from the 9th to the 15th century, the heyday of the Jewish settlement in Girona.

CATHEDRAL ●

This is one of the most impressive churches in Spain. Work has been carried out on the *Santa Maria* church from the 14th century almost to the present day. At 23m/75ft it has the widest nave of any Gothic church in Europe. The 16th century high altar is made of silver and set with gem stones. No fewer than 30 side chapels with precious paintings surround the cloister inside. And the church holds lots of other treasures, such as a 12th century tapestry *Mon–Fri 10am–8pm, Sat 10am–4.30pm, Sun 2pm–8pm | admission 5 euros | Plaça de la Catedral | www.catedraldegirona.org*

MUSEU DEL CINE

The museum exhibits 8000 items in an area of more than half an acre: from the camera which belonged to the Lumière brothers to film equipment. There is also a specialist library. *Tue–Fri 10am–6pm, Sat 10am–8pm, Sun 11am–3pm | admission 5 euros | Carrer Sèquia, 1 | www.museu delcinema.org*

MUSEU D'HISTÒRIA DE LA CIUTAT

Here you can follow the whole history of the town in one go. *Tue–Sat 10am–2pm and 5pm–7pm | admission 4 euros | Carrer de la Força, 27 | www.ajuntament.gi/museu_ciutat*

WALK ON THE TOWN WALLS ☼

Start behind the cathedral at *Portal de Sant Cristóbal,* and head south. For almost a mile you will be able to enjoy a good view of the town.

FOOD & DRINK

BOIRA

This is a tapas bar with unusual tapas and a restaurant with Mediterranean food. If you get there in good time, you will enjoy a good ☼ **INSIDER TIP** view of the Rio Onyar with the colourful house facades opposite. *Daily | Pl. Independència, 17 | tel. 9 72 21 96 05 | Budget*

CAFÉ CONTEXT LLIBERIA

In this old town café, much frequented by students, you will find books, subdued music and young intellectuals – or those who think they are – and you can try their speciality, a croque monsieur. *Daily | Pou Rodó, 21 | tel. 9 72 48 63 90 | www.cafe context.com | Budget*

EL BALCÓ

Argentinian restaurant serving first class grilled steaks. There is also a great selection of Argentinian wines. *Closed Sun | C/ Hortes, 16 | tel. 9 72 22 31 61 | www.elbalco restaurant.net | Moderate*

The Bellmirall guesthouse in Girona's old town is a cosy, charming place with lots of character

INSIDER TIP ▶ EL CELLER DE CAN ROCA ☺
This restaurant is run by the Girona Bons Fogons cookery collective. The emphasis is on traditional food and the use of local market produce. They are famous for their *lluç am vinagreta d'alls i romaní*: sole in vinaigrette with rosemary and garlic. *Closed Sun and Mon | Can Sunyer, 46 | tel. 9 72 22 21 57 | www.cellercanroca.com | Expensive*

SHOPPING

ULYSSUS BOOKSHOP
Books (also in English) and maps (hiking) for travellers to stock up on. *Carrer Ballesteries, 29*

ENTERTAINMENT

It is all rather quiet in Girona in the late evening. There are a few small bars and cafés in the old town.

BAR PLATEA
This former theatre is an evening meeting place for Girona's students. *From 8pm |* Carrer Jeroni Real de Fontclara, 4 | tel. 9 72 22 72 88 | www.localplatea.com

SUNSET JAZZ CLUB
Girona's jazz club is in the old town, there is a changing live programme of national and international bands. *Daily | Pons i Martí, 12 | www.sunsetjazz-club.com*

WHERE TO STAY

BELLMIRALL
This is a very comfortable guesthouse in the old town with a pleasant ambience. *7 rooms | Bellmirall, 3 | tel. 9 72 20 40 09 | Moderate*

HOTEL CONDAL
This hotel enjoys a central location, the rooms are bright and comfortable, and there are frequent special offers. *28 rooms | C/Joan Maragall, 10 | tel. 9 72 20 44 62 | www.hotelcondalgirona.com | Budget*

HOTEL HISTÒRIC
The walls of this hotel date back to the year 1000. The furniture in the rooms is

individually made by the owners them-selves. *9 rooms | Bellmirall, 4 | tel. 9 72 22 35 83 | www.hotelhistoric.com | Expensive*

LLORET DE MAR

(124 B–C5) *(₥ D12)* ★ ● **For some the ultimate amusement paradise, for others a monument to cheap pleasure and bad taste.**

What is certain is that no other place on the Costa Brava has shaped the image of this region to such an extent as Lloret (pop. 15,000). The Romans were once here, at which time the place had the romantic name Lauretum, due to the laurels which grew in abundance here. Thanks to the 5km/3mi long beach and a boisterous entertainment business which goes on round the clock, the number of inhabitants easily exceeds 100,000 in summer.

INFORMATION

OFICINA MUNICIPAL DE TURISME
Rambla de la Llibertat, 1 | tel. 9 72 22 65 75 | www.ajuntament.gi/turisme

WHERE TO GO

INSIDER TIP ▶ **CALDES DE MALAVELLA** ●
(124 B3) *(₥ C10)*
To get to these thermal baths (approx. 17km/10mi south of Girona) you can save yourself the motorway toll and take the perfectly ● good NII/A2. Here you can purchase the healing spa water and two hotels also offer anti-stress and beauty treatments and various massages. If you are looking for relaxation, you will find comfortable accommodation in an old villa *Balnear i Prats (76 rooms | Plaça Sant Esteve, 7 | tel. 9 72 47 00 51 | www.balneari prats.com | Expensive)*.

SANT DANIEL MONASTERY ●
(122 A4) *(₥ C8)*
A 3km/2mi drive through the beautiful Sant Daniel valley leads to the Benedictine Sant Daniel Monastery, which is now oc-cupied by nuns. St Daniel's tomb is to be found here. In addition to the 11th cen-tury church, the INSIDER TIP ▶ two-storey cloister, above Gothic, below Romanesque, is worth seeing. *2km/1mi from the town outskirts*

SANT PERE DE GALLIGANTS
(122 A4) *(₥ C8)*
The 10th century Benedictine monastery is, with its octagonal tower, one of the purest Romanesque buildings in the prov-ince. *Plaça de Santa Llúcia on the town outskirts*

SIGHTSEEING

CASA DE LA VILA
The town hall, built in 1872 in a mix of Art Nouveau and neoclassicism, is on the beach promenade and is surrounded by palms.

CENTRO CULTURAL VERDAGUER

There is an exhibition of paintings by Catalan artists and model ships in this villa built in 1887. It also puts on readings, concerts, lectures and changing exhibitions. *Tue–Sun 11am–1pm and 4pm–8pm | admission free | Passeig Jacint Verdaguer, s/n*

DONA MARINERA ☼

A monument for the wives of the fishermen of Lloret, the bronze statue by the Catalan sculptor Ernest Maragall portrays a woman greeting the returning boats. *At the southern end of Lloret beach*

ESGLÉSIA DE SANT ROMÀ

The most important church in Lloret dates from the early 16th century, but has been constantly changed and extended. The church roof is covered with patterns of coloured tiles. *Plaça d'Església*

MUSEU DEL MAR

Pictures, documents and models show the historic relationship of Lloret to the sea and also, for example, to maritime trade and fishing. *June–Sept Mon–Sat 10am–1pm and 4pm–8pm, Sun 10am–1pm and 4pm–7pm, Oct/Nov Mon–Sat 9am–1pm and 4pm–7pm, Sun 10am–1pm and 4pm–7pm, Dec–Feb Mon–Sat 9am–1.30pm and 3.30pm–6pm, Sun 9am–2pm, March–May Mon–Sat 9am–1pm and 4pm–7pm, Sun 10am–1pm and 4pm–7pm | admission 4 euros | Passeig Campodron i Arrieta, 1–2*

PASEO DE MAR ☼

A stroll along the palm-lined beach promenade leads past the town hall and stately 19th century town houses, behind the promenade you will still find some 16th century buildings in the old town's narrow streets.

SANTA CRISTINA

Each year on 24 July, the 18th century chapel with an Italian marble altar is the starting point of a procession of boats bearing the figure of St Christina. *Platja de Santa Cristina (signposted)*

FOOD & DRINK

There are countless bars, fast food shops, cheap restaurants, but also restaurants serving sophisticated cuisine.

Beach life: Lloret de Mar has shaped the image of the Costa Brava like no other place

Lloret's nightlife pulsates in the discos

veal or poached oysters. The rooms are spacious, though for some tastes perhaps rather too mundane. *Closed Sun evening and Mon | Ctra. de Tossa, s/n | tel. 9 72 36 93 26 | www.freurestaurant.com | Expensive*

CAN TARRADAS

This restaurant offers value for money with good home cooking and traditional dishes such as paella and fish. They have a wide range of Spanish wines from every region. *Daily | Plaça d'Espanya, 7 | tel. 9 72 37 06 02 | www.restaurantecantarradas. com | Budget*

EL TRULL

The finest seafood is served, including paella and a wide range of salads. There are 15 different menus. *Daily | Plaça Nacions Unides, 1 | tel. 9 72 36 49 28 | www.eltrull. com | Expensive*

INSIDERTIP FREU 😊

A trio of young chefs, Núria Camps, Pep Arbós and Nacho Arregui, are committed to classical Mediterranean food. In addition to seasonal market produce, the food is also creative, for example roast leg of

SHOPPING

In Lloret the emphasis is on value for money items, everything from trendy sunglasses to decorated T-shirts. The market day is Tuesday in *Carrer Senia de Rabic.*

SPORTS, ACTIVITIES & BEACHES

The following beaches are ideal for children: *Cala Canyelles* a bay north of the town, surrounded by rocks, with coarse-grained sand, showers and kiosk; the town beach *Platja de Lloret*, more than 1km long, is very busy at all times of the day and has rather coarse-grained sand and a complete range of facilities; and there are two bays next to one another, *Platja de Santa Cristina y Treumal* separated by rocks, with coarse sand, clean water, showers and kiosk.

DIVING

Lessons are available and you can hire equipment at *Nauti Sub Lloret | Ronda d'Europe 4pm–6pm | tel. 9 72 37 26 41, tel. mobile 6 95 16 20 08 | www.nautisub.net*

ENTERTAINMENT

Lloret is famous for its night life. Most discos and bars are located in the streets behind the town hall.

CASINO LLORET

You can win and or lose at roulette, baccarat and on the one-armed bandits. *Daily 5pm–4am | Carrer dels Esports, 1 | tel. 9 72 36 65 12*

COLOSSOS

Of the approx. 30 discos, this is one of the most popular. It opens late and closes late. Variety of music including hip hop, house and salsa. *Daily | admission dependent on music | Avinguda Just Marlès, 38 | tel. 972 36 51 76 | www.disco colossos.com*

WHERE TO STAY

HOTEL ACAPULCO

Large, centrally located, family-friendly with two swimming pools and a children's playground. *200 rooms | Carrer Josep de Togores, 21 | tel. 972 36 54 98 | www.hotel acapulcolloret.com | Moderate*

HOTEL MIRAMAR

Here you will find simply everything you need – from the beach to the well equipped fitness centre. *54 rooms | Passeig Jacint Verdaguer, 6 | tel. 972 36 47 62 | www. hotelmiramarlloret.com | Expensive*

HOTEL ROGER DE FLOR PALACE

Located in a historic building away from all the hustle and bustle, the hotel offers a bar, restaurant, swimming pool and all creature comforts. *93 rooms | Turó de L'Estat, s/n | tel. 972 36 48 00 | www.hotel rogerdeflorpalace.com | Moderate*

HOTEL SANTA MARTA

This hotel enjoys a quiet location in a small wood by the Santa Cristina beach. The rooms are spacious and either have park or sea views. *76 rooms | Platja Santa Cristina, s/n | tel. 972 36 49 04 | www. hotelsantamarta.net | Expensive*

INFORMATION

OFICINA D'INFORMACIÓ TURÍSTICA

Passeig Campodron, 1 | tel. 972 36 47 35 | www.lloret.org

WHERE TO GO

JARDINES DE SANTA CLOTILDE ●
(124 B5) (🗺 D12)

The Santa Clotilde Gardens, laid out in 1919, are located above the beach 3km/2mi south of Lloret. The shady park has tall trees and Mediterranean flora, paths, statues and a splendid, privately owned villa. *April–Sept Tue–Sun 10am–8pm, Oct–March Tue–Sun 10am–5pm | admission 3 euros*

TOSSA DE MAR

🗺 MAP ON PAGE 127
(125 D4) (🗺 D–E12) ★ When the Russian painter Marc Chagall visited Tossa in 1933, he called it 'the blue paradise'.

Decades before the huge tourist boom, Tossa had a great attraction for artists, no doubt because of its beautiful location on a bay, and it's an unspoilt medieval town. The town's four fine, sandy beaches today attract tourists who prefer a more informal, less structured holiday. According to local statistics, 65 per cent of visiting families often return again and again.

Tossa is also popular with the Catalans, and at weekends you will see more people from Barcelona than in the other coastal resorts. Since tourism is not so intensively developed as elsewhere, Tossa (pop. about 3300) has been able to preserve its identity to this day.

SIGHTSEEING

MUSEU MUNICIPAL

The town museum is housed the former Governor's Palace, a 14th century building on the edge of the old town. Here lots of original works by major artists are exhibited, especially painters who spent some time in Tossa – such as Marc Chagall, André Masson and Olga Sacharow. In the archaeological section you can see a 4th century floor mosaic as well as other finds from the Roman period. *June–Sept Tue–Fri 10am–2pm and 4pm–6pm, Sat and Sun 10am–3pm, Oct–May Tue–Fri 11am–1pm and 3pm–5pm, Sat and Sun 11am–5pm | admission 3 euros | Plaça Roig i Soler, 1*

VILA VELLA
The old town is a piece of the Middle Ages in the heart of Tossa. The defence walls – erected in the 11th century for protection against pirates – and the houses are still intact. Around 80 of the houses are even still inhabited. The old town is today a tourist magnet – thanks to comprehensive restoration work between 1923 and 1990. Only the 15th century church perched on a hill is still in ruins. Narrow alleys lead to the top of the ☀ hill, from where there is a magnificent view of the coast.

FOOD & DRINK

CAN PINI
The paella and fish dishes served here are highly recommended, especially the *dorada a la sal*, sea bream in salt. *Daily | Portal, 14 | tel. 972 34 02 97 | www.canpini.com | Moderate*

LA CUINA DE CAN SIMON ☺
Young chefs from the *joves cuiners* cookery collective do the cooking here. The emphasis is on Catalan cuisine, enhanced with creative trends and the use of regional produce. The restaurant is attractively done out in reddish colours but there are only 22 places. *Closed Sun evening, Mon and Tue | C/del Portal, 24 | tel. 972 34 12 69 | Expensive*

MARINA
The restaurant with terrace is located in a side street and its speciality is paella. *Sept–May closed Mon and Tue | Carrer Tarull, 6 | tel. 972 34 07 57 | Budget*

SANTA MARTA
In the heart of the old town, this restaurant concentrates on fish and paella, and their speciality is INSIDER TIP *cim-i-tomba*, skate, potatoes and *allioli*, prepared differently from place to place. *Daily | C/ Francesc de Paula Aromi, 2 | tel. 972 34 04 72 | Expensive*

SHOPPING

WEEKLY MARKET
A clothes market with some fruit and vegetable stalls is held on Thursdays from 8am–2pm. *Avinguda Joan Maragall*

SPORTS, ACTIVITIES & BEACHES

BEACHES
Tossa has three beaches within easy reach: *Platja Gran* and *Platja del Reig* in front of the town, and *Platja de Mar Menuda* on the northern outskirts. These beaches are clean and relatively well equipped. However, this cannot be said for *Es Codolar*, the small beach below Vila Vella: when it is windy, all sorts of refuse collects in the bay.

DIVING
Lessons and equipment hire are available at: *Centro de Submarinismo Mar Menuda | Platja de Mar Menuda, s/n | tel. 972 34 16 39 | www.divingtossa.com*

HIKING
You can pick up information about the various hikes into the mountainous hinterland from the tourist office *(www.info tossa.com, see right).*

Tossa de Mar: beach life against a medieval backdrop

WATER SPORTS

Offering everything for the water sports enthusiast – sailing, surfing, kayaking, water skiing and diving – at *Cala Llevadó Water Sports Centre. Ctra. Lloret, 3km/ 2mi | tel. 9 72 34 18 66 | www.cll-water-sports.com*

ENTERTAINMENT

Bars and restaurants are located in *Carrer Portal*.

WHERE TO STAY

DIANA

For many people this is the nicest hotel in the town. In a 100 year old building, all the rooms have beautifully tiled floors and some also have Art Nouveau furniture. *21 rooms | Plaça de España, 6 | tel. 9 72 34 18 86 | www.diana-hotel.com | Moderate–Expensive*

HOSTAL D'ALBA

This guesthouse enjoys a central location and represents good value for money. The rooms are small, but all have a shower and some have a balcony. *21 rooms | C/Giverola, 3 | tel. 9 72 34 08 59 | Budget*

INFORMATION

OFICINA MUNICIPAL DE TURISME

Avinguda de Pelegrí 25 (by the bus station) | tel. 9 72 34 01 08 | www.infotossa.com

WHERE TO GO

There are numerous bays in the immediate vicinity where you can spend a wonderful sunny day alternating between beach and sea. If you head north there is *Cala Bona (3km /2mi)*, *Cala Pola (4km/2.5mi)* and *Cala Giverola (5km/3mi)*; if you head south, there is *Cala Llevadó (3km/2mi)* and *Cala Morisca (5km/3mi)*.

BARCELONA

MAP INSIDE BACK COVER
(0) *(Ⓜ 0)*

Barcelona, the capital of the autonomous region of Catalonia, is situated only a

> **CITY** **WHERE TO START?**
> Take a stroll along *Las Ramblas*. From **Plaça Catalunya** *(Metro: Plaça de Catalunya)* to the port, plane trees line the sides and in the middle performers provide entertainment, presenting themselves to the public in countless different guises. You are best advised to leave the car at home!

stone's throw from the Costa Brava. It is a very lively, cosmopolitan city.

Culture, science and economics have brought the city (pop. 2 million) international recognition and the 1992 Olympics helped it achieve worldwide fame.

You will find everything you need to know about Barcelona in the MARCO POLO 'Barcelona' travel guide.

SIGHTSEEING

Many sights can be reached on foot and those further out quite easily by the Metro or bus. There is also the *Bus Turístic* which stops at many tourist attractions on

Photo: Palau de la Música Catalana

Art Nouveau buildings, bustling squares, elegant boulevards and narrow alleyways – Barcelona an exciting and vibrant city

its tour round the city. *Daily from 9am from Plaça de Catalunya | www.barcelonabus turistic.cat | day ticket 26 euros (children 15 euros), 34 euros for 2 consecutive days*

BARCELONETA (U E5–6) *(ﾉﾉ e5–6)*

The former fishing quarter is a popular destination for a Sunday excursion. There is plenty of atmosphere, the washing flutters in the wind in the narrow streets and

there is a smell of fish. The beach is situated close by, and lots of buildings have been renovated.

BARRI GÒTIC (U D3–4) *(ﾉﾉ d3–4)*

The Gothic quarter is the heart of Barcelona. Take a stroll through the narrow streets and you can have a look in *colmadas,* corner shops, and pubs with very reasonable lunchtime menus. In recent years t'ai chi

Consecrated by the pope as a *basilica minor*: Antoni Gaudí's Sagrada Família Cathedral

centres and esoteric shops have also opened in this area. But the sounds of the knife grinders still resonate through the streets.

BOQUERIA ● (U C4) *(ⓜ c4)*
In the city's best known market hall, you will find the most mouth-watering display of the entire culinary offer from the local land and sea. You can try out tapas and wines in the market bars.

CATEDRAL (U D3) *(ⓜ d3)*
Work began on building Barcelona's Gothic cathedral in 1298 but it was only completed in the 15th century. Rather unusually for a church, there are geese swimming on a pond in the palm lined courtyard. *Daily 8am–1.30pm and 5pm–7.30pm | admission 5 euros | Plaça de la Seu*

LA PEDRERA (U D1) *(ⓜ d1)*
One of the outstanding examples of *modernismo* architecture, designed by Gaudí in 1910 and his last work before he dedicated himself to the Sagrada Familia. The composition is a residential building with a curved facade, with recessed balconies. There are lots of details to admire, such as the roof sculptures, the ironwork on the doors, and the balconies. Today **INSIDER TIP** parts of the building can be visited, including an apartment in the *modernismo* style. *Daily Nov–Feb 9am–6.30pm, March–Oct 9am–8pm | admission 10 euros | Passeig de Gràcia, 92*

MUSEU D'ART CONTEMPORANI (U C3) *(ⓜ c3)*
The modern 1995 museum building in the middle of the old district of Raval is not to be missed. The architecture alone makes a visit worthwhile, and the museum houses a permanent exhibition of some 2000 works by contemporary artists, as well as rooms for temporary exhibitions and cultural events. *Sept–June Mon/Wed–Fri 11am–7.30pm, Sat 10am–8pm, Sun 10am–3pm, July–Sept 11am–8pm Sat 10am–8pm and Sun 10am–3pm | admission 7.50 euros | Plaça dels Àngels | www.macba.cat*

MUSEU PICASSO (U E4) (𝄞 e4)

Some of the most important collections of the artistic genius are displayed in this museum: works from the blue and pink periods. Temporary exhibitions are also regularly held. *Tue–Sun 10am–8pm | admission 9 euros | Carrer Montcada, 3–23 | www.museupicasso.bcn.es*

PALAU DE LA MÚSICA CATALANA (U E3) (𝄞 e3)

This splendid Art Nouveau masterpiece was built from 1905–08. Catalan Art Nouveau, also known as *modernismo*, finds its extravagant high point in this building. Concerts are frequently held, from classical to pop to folk music. *Closed except for concerts | C/Sant Pere Més Alt, s/n | www.palaumusica.org*

PARC DE LA CIUTADELA (U F4) (𝄞 f4)

This large park was laid out in 1860 on a former military site as a pleasure park for the city residents. It has lakes where you can go on a boat trip, and historic buildings designed for the 1888 World Exhibition by architects of *modernismo* such as Lluis Domènech and Gaudí. Today they are used for various purposes, such as the *Geological Museum*. The *Zoo* is also accommodated here. *Daily 8am–sunset | admission free | Passeig de Pujades, s/n*

PARC GÜELL ☁ (0) (𝄞 0)

Antoni Gaudí actually intended to create a completely new city district here. But what arose is a wonderful park with colonnades like sea waves, statues and mosaic benches. The park is very popular. *Daily 10am–7pm, in summer 10am–9pm | Carrer d'Olot | Metro: Lesseps*

RAMBLAS ★ (U C5–D3) (𝄞 c5–d3)

The most visited section of the famous boulevard starts at Plaça de Catalunya and ends just before the port by the Columbus Monument. Beneath tall plane trees flower sellers, cartoonists, newspaper sellers and small pet dealers display their wares whilst street artists pose as living statues. In recent years Las Ramblas has lost a great deal of its former charm due to the tacky shops, the high incidence of pick pocketing and theft and prostitution.

SAGRADA FAMÍLIA ★ (U F1) (𝄞 f1)

The still unfinished cathedral is an outstanding example of the building style of Antoni Gaudí, Catalonia's most famous architect. Work has been progressing on the Sagrada Familia for more than 120 years. But lack of funds mean that the spectacular building is still surrounded by scaffolding and cranes. Approx. 50 per cent of the building is unfinished, including ten towers, some of which are supposed to be 170m/560ft high. *April–Sept daily 9am–8pm, Oct–March daily 9am–6pm | admission 12 euros | Carrer Mallorca, 401 | www.sagradafamilia.org*

FOOD & DRINK

ARÀNEGA (U B4) (𝄞 b4)

First class Catalan cuisine is served in this former dairy. The homemade desserts such as INSIDER TIP ▶ *crema catalana* are outstanding. *Closed Mon | Avingudra Parallel, 188 | tel. 9 33 25 63 07 | Budget*

★ **Ramblas**
The famous boulevard is full of life until late at night
→ p. 85

★ **Sagrada Família**
Antoni Gaudí's spectacular cathedral – still unfinished
→ p. 85

MARCO POLO HIGHLIGHTS

Enjoying Barcelona: specialities from the coast with a panoramic view of port and beach

INSIDER TIP **GRANJA LA PALLARESA** ●
(U D4) (ω d4)

The former dairy dating from 1947 was turned into a traditional café and has catered for whole generations in Barcelona. The speciality is *churros*, a fried dough pastry, and the correct way to eat it is to dip it in sweet, thick hot chocolate. Another speciality is *suizo* (the Swiss): hot chocolate topped with cream. *Daily | C/Petritxol,11 | tel. 9 33 02 20 36*

RESTAURANT MONDO ❧
(U D5) (ω d5)

Bernat Bermundo, the renowned head chef at this restaurant with terrace and a view of the port, places the emphasis on fresh produce, especially with seafood which is mainly prepared the Galician way. *Closed Mon | Moll d'Espanya, s/n | tel. 9 32 21 39 11 | Expensive*

TAFI (U D1) (ω d1)

This is where the gaucho can eat in a rustic Argentinean atmosphere. It is a steakhouse serving every kind of steak, Argentinean wines and desserts. *Closed Sun | Còrsega, 68 | Moderate*

INSIDER TIP **TANTARANTANA**
(U E4) (ω e4)

Serving food fresh from the market, such as sweet potato *(boniato)* vol-au-vents with egg and mushrooms. The stone walls and the ceiling beams create a pleasant contrast to the otherwise modern furnishings. *Closed Sun | C/Tantarantana, 24 | tel. 9 32 68 24 10 | Moderate*

SHOPPING

Many streets are dominated by the same type of shop. Antiques in the *Barri Gòtic*, especially in *Carrer Banys Nous* (U D4) (ω d4); antiquarian books in the *Barri Gòtic* (U D3–4) (ω d3–4); fashion in *Passeig de Gràcia* (U D2–3) (ω d2–3); art in *Carrer Montcada* in the area around the Picasso Museum (U E4) (ω e4); wine and food in *Boquería* (U C4) (ω c4); and shoes in *Carrer de Pelai* and *Portal de l'Àngel* (U D3) (ω d3).

INSIDER TIP ▶ ALTAÏR BOOKSHOP
(U D2) (*d2*)

This is Spain's best bookshop for travel books, from guide books to travelogues in English. It is a great place for browsing. *Gran Via, 616 | www.altair.es*

ENTERTAINMENT

GRAN TEATRE DEL LICEU
(U C4) (*c4*)

The elegant opera house has been renovated after a fire in the 1990s. It puts on splendid productions with an international cast. *Ramblas/Carrer Sant Pau | tel. 9 34 85 99 00 | www.liceubarcelona.com*

LONDON BAR ● (U C4) (*c4*)

Hippies and literary figures, such as Orwell and Hemingway, used to meet here in the Franco era. Now it is mostly a place where free live concerts are held almost every day. *Carrer Nou de La Rambla, 34 | tel. 9 33 18 52 61 | www.londonbarbcn.com*

MARSELLA (U C4) (*c4*)

The rather faded restaurant has now been modernised. The metal tables are modern and the toilets have undergone a facelift. All in all: an absinth bar with an off-beat clientele. *Closed Sun | C/ Sant Pau, 65*

RAZZMATAZZ (0) (*0*)

One of the most well-known and popular clubs in the city. International bands and DJs appear and there is a wide range of music. At the weekend there is dancing on five floors. *Daily | C/Pamplona, 88*

WHERE TO STAY

HOSTAL GOYA (U D3) (*d3*)

The guesthouse enjoys a central location and also has two apartments (with kitchen) to rent. The style is modern, the rooms bright and comfortable. *19 rooms | C/Pau de Caris, 74 | tel. 9 33 02 25 65 | www.hostal goya.com | Moderate*

HOTEL CLIMENT (0) (*0*)

Good value for money, clean and handy for connections to the airport, railway station and Metro, basic rooms. *35 rooms | Gran Via Corts Catalanes, 304 | tel. 9 33 23 98 07 | www.hotelcliment.com | Budget*

HOTEL ESPAÑA (U C4) (*c4*)

In the immediate vicinity of Las Ramblas, this is a well-established hotel with Art Nouveau furnishings and a large, reasonably priced restaurant. *80 rooms | Carrer Sant Pau, 1pm–4pm and 8pm–11pm | tel. 9 33 18 17 58 | www.hotelespanya.com | Expensive*

INFORMATION

TURISME DE BARCELONA
(U D3) (*d3*)

Plaça de Catalunya, 17 | in the basement | tel. 9 06 30 12 82 | www.barcelonaturisme. com

LOW BUDGET

▶ Whilst a single trip on the Metro costs 2 euros, the price for a ten-trip ticket is only 9.25 euros for one zone.

▶ You can eat very reasonably at lunchtime in the city's market halls. A three-course menu costs only 8 euros in the *Mercat de Sant Antoni (Carrer Comte d'Urgell)* or in the *Mercat de Galvany (Carrer Santaló, 65)*. This does not apply, however, to the mother of all markets, the *Boqueria (see p. 83)*. The *Barceloneta* market hall is also good value for money.

TRIPS & TOURS

The tours are marked in green in the road atlas, the pull-out map and on the back cover

1 IN THE TRANQUIL HINTERLAND

You should allow a whole day for this round trip of some 80km/50mi through the hinterland. The towns – hardly any of them have more than 8000 inhabitants – are a reflection of the local way of living. Even if it does not look a long way, bear in mind that the roads are often narrow and winding, and there are all sorts of things to explore on the way.

The trip starts in L'Escala → p. 41. It is a nice idea to set off from the old town after enjoying an early morning coffee and a fine view of the sea. But you should get going as soon as possible to call in at the picturesque market in La Bisbal → p. 54, the first stop on the route and one definitely not to be missed. The market there is open on Fridays from 8am. The country road via Verges takes you through farmland and crosses the Ter and the Daró, two rivers which keep the land fertile. As you drive into La Bisbal on the main street you will pass one ceramics shop after another. You are well advised to take the first free parking space you see and to continue on foot to the market in the old town. The lively market is held in the shade of the

Stunning bays and ancient ruins: a round trip through towns in the interior and a drive along the coast with great views

mighty Bishop's Palace. There is always a lot going on: women testing the ripeness of the fruit, men discussing the latest football results, market traders slicing their sausages, and teenagers examining the latest T-shirt designs.

After the market you can visit the nearby Palau de la Bisbal, the Bishop's Palace, and see how a bishop used to live in the Middle Ages: there is a kitchen, wine cel-

lar, stables, store rooms and the palace prison. You should also definitely have a browse in the ceramics shops on the main street. Though it is true that only a few of the items come directly from the town, the selection of beautiful pottery for everyday use is absolutely huge.

From La Bisbal the route takes you to Palafrugell → p. 60, 10km/6mi on the C66, a highway with occasionally heavy traffic. Palafrugell is one of those towns with narrow streets where it is best to park your car as soon as possible and continue on foot. You can pick up a town map at the tourist office. The town centre is small and it is easy to find your way about. The **Cork Museum → p. 61** is worth a visit and it is easy to find if you keep your eyes on the large metal tower rising up above the houses. You should then call in at the **Casino** on Plaça Nova. The atmosphere

the coast lying below Begur from the ☆ **Mirador Sant Roman** or from the ☆ **Castell**. If you now want to be at the sea, then it is well worth driving the few miles down to **Aiguablava → p. 54**. The small bay has marvellously clear water, though it can get very busy in summer. Back in Begur, you drive about 5km/3mi on the country road 653 till you rejoin the C 31 and, heading north, you come to **Pals → p. 54** after a further 4km/2.5mi.

The beautifully restored streets of Pals offer a trip back to the Middle Ages

there resembles a large, cool and relaxing waiting room, with old age pensioners sitting quietly and businessmen hard at work on their phones. Simply enjoy the very special atmosphere.

A diversion heading north takes you via the C31 to **Begur → p. 50**. The 7km/4mi drive to get there is absolutely worthwhile: the small town radiates calm, with no hustle and bustle, and locals get together over a coffee on the church square. You can enjoy a lovely panoramic view of

Here you must leave your car at the car park outside the town. The walled town, perched on a hill, transports you straight back into the Middle Ages – the only difference being that now everything is beautifully maintained and preserved. This has earned the town some prizes, including the Spanish National Prize for Fine Arts.

The Romanesque **Església Sant Pere** is worth seeing, decorated with a Baroque gate and located on a picturesque square.

Some restaurants have also set up in the medieval walls. Should you already be feeling a bit peckish, then try the Can Bonet *(Carrer Samaria, 55 | tel. 9 72 66 73 42 | Budget)*, where there is good local food.

After you have had a bite to eat, it is worth paying a visit to Sa Punta, the long beach in Pals. The drive continues on the GIV6502 steadily downhill, past the holiday resort of Els Masos de Pals – which was once a showpiece town project – and you then come to the coast after just over 5km/3mi. To the right is ☼ Cap de Forn and a trip there provides a magnificent view of the sea. If you look to the north, however, you will be able to make out the miles of Sa Punta beach and the forest of red and white aerials. The twelve aerials are part of the former Radio Liberty station, a US broadcaster from the time of the Cold War when the eastern block was bombarded with western propaganda from here. It all looks rather utopian, but as you get nearer this impression fades as you observe the bathers having fun on the wide beach, and the apartment buildings, which are often used as second homes by local people. The occasionally severe north wind and the sandy seabed attracts wind surfers. The River Ter flows into the sea at the north of the beach, leaving behind alluvial sand – a paradise for sea birds. Beyond the river there is another beach. If by now you have had enough of beach life, then you can drive back to the road and head for Pals, whose name is said to derive from the Latin *palus*, meaning in Spanish *pantanoso*, swamp area.

From Pals it is around 10km/6mi via the C 31 to Torroella de Montgrí → p. 66. This town with its 5600 inhabitants has been smartened up in recent years, creating the atmosphere of an authentic Spanish town, and is worth a longer stay. You can spend many a pleasant hour just in the Can Quintana → p. 66, the Mediterranean Culture Centre housed in a former palace. Particularly interesting are the **INSIDER TIP** audio stations with numerous musical examples from the countries around the Mediterranean.

It is also worth taking a walk along Carrer de l'Església. The street leads not only to the imposing Església de Sant Genís, a 14th century Gothic church, but also to the exclusive hotel and restaurant, Palau Lo Mirador → p. 68. If you are shocked by the equally exclusive prices, then you can at least cast a glance inside at the elegant furnishings and impressive architecture and admire the beautiful gardens. After L'Escala it is via the C31 and GI632 for approx. 12km/7mi.

2 PARTY ANIMALS AND SMALL FISH

It is hard to imagine any tour of the Costa Brava which could be as rich in contrasts as this one: around the clock party mood in Lloret de Mar and fish auctions in Palamós. Whereas in the major tourist resorts, such as Lloret de Mar and Platja d'Aro, it is all about pleasure seeking day and night, the fishermen of Palamós look anxiously at the computer screen to find out what today's catch has yielded. The tour starts in Lloret de Mar, goes along the coast via Tossa de Mar to Sant Feliu de Guíxols and ends in Palamós where, from 5pm on working days, the daily fish auction begins in the port in the *La Llotja* auction hall. Though the whole tour only covers some 62km/ 40mi, it has it all, especially the 10km/ 6mi long ☼ part of the route north of Tossa, a winding stretch of road with frequent stops to enjoy its many viewing points.

In the morning when there are still a few scattered party animals recovering in the cafés which have opened up early, you can enjoy a rare sight in Lloret de Mar → p. 76: the beach is almost empty, with just a few joggers running alongside the sea. Otherwise it all looks rather desolate: litter blowing around, delivery vans parked outside restaurants, and the shops only gradually starting to open.

So, it is now back to the car and off into the country. You head north on the GI 682 which wends its way far from the sea round tight bends up into the mountains. After 13km/8mi you come back down to the coast and to Tossa de Mar → p. 79. From the old part of the town, the ☀ Vila Vella, you have a lovely view of the morning coast. The Museu Municipal → p. 79, located at the foot of the old town, is open from 10am. The exhibition of paintings by Marc Chagall, which the artist painted in the light of Tossa, makes a charming complement to the actual picture which is just beginning to emerge outside before your very eyes.

If you then climb up the narrow streets of the old town, you may again feel as though you are in a museum. But people actually live here. After a walk of about 15 minutes you come to the ☀ INSIDER TIP lighthouse which is an ideal picnic spot and also a great view. Before leaving the town, you can still enjoy a swim at Platja del Reig. This small bay is situated below Avinguda Sant Ramón, almost exactly opposite the Vila Vella.

From Tossa heading north, the GI 682 begins to climb once more. Take care on the ☀ tight hairpin bends, it is best to pull over into one of the lay-bys rather than try to enjoy the view of the coast whilst you are driving. And this view is really magnificent. In the morning the sea shines in a clear blue, out at sea fishing boats sail past in the white wake, and

beneath the road lovely bathing bays beckon.

From the small village of Salionç the road again heads away from the sea until (after 13km/8mi) you reach Sant Feliu de Guíxols → p. 63. The town with 15,000 inhabitants is a popular beach resort, but it is all much calmer and quieter than in Lloret de Mar. There is a lovely seaside promenade and it is about 500m from Plaça de Sant Pere to the nautical club. Above is ☀ El Fortim, a building in which equipment for rescuing shipwrecked sailors is kept: a place of peace and quiet with lovely views of the bay of Sant Felíu and the bustling fishing port.

On the way back there are some lovely Art Nouveau buildings to admire: Casa Patxot with a really beautiful sundial on its facade and Casino dels Nois dating from 1889. Like most casinos in Spain, this is also a nice place to enjoy a relaxing cup of coffee. You can also gain an overview of the region's prehistoric past in the Museu Municipal (June–Sept Tue–Sun 10am–1pm and 5pm–8pm, Oct–May Tue–Sun 11am–2pm and 4pm–7pm | admission free | Plaça Monestir). The museum has an exhibition of coins, weapons and ceramics from the Roman period.

The next stop only 5km/3mi away is Platja d'Aro → p. 61 where there is no great difference from Lloret de Mar. There is the same type and range of beach facilities for tourists, with bars, mass-produced goods and hordes of people on the streets. Continuing the tour, driving north, you first pass some holiday homes, pine trees obscuring most of the view of the sea. Just beyond Platja d'Aro you then descend to sea level again.

8km/5mi further you are welcomed by a less intrusive atmosphere: Palamós → p. 57, the last stop on this tour and in many respects one of its highlights. There is parking right next to the beach in the town centre. What immediately catches your eye is the large fishing port and its long breakwater. With a bit of luck you might also be able to see INSIDER TIP the fishermen mending their nets. You can now, depending on the time of day, first of all wander along Paseo Marítimo, call in at one of the cafés or go down into the town. In Carrer Mayor it is usually pretty busy and the range of goods is, in comparison with other places on the Costa

the nearby *La Llotja,* the fish auction hall. All that now remains is to enhance your knowledge of fishing, which you can best do in the Museu de la Pesca → p. 57 situated right next to *La llotja* in the port. There is nowhere else where you can get a better understanding of the cycle of fish, catch and food than in this museum. If you are now feeling a bit hungry, you can round off the trip in one of Palamós' good fish restaurants, for example in the Club

Shop talk: in the port town of Palamós everything revolves around fishing

Brava, less tailored for tourists. You will find mainly Catalan food, shoes and outdoor clothing.

If you are here in the afternoon, on no account must you miss the arrival of the fishing boats, which is usually from about 4pm. They enter the port accompanied by shrieking of the seagulls, and on board are the crates with the catch already on ice. You should then go straight over to

Nautic → p. 57, an exclusive club, with restaurant, for sailors and other water sports enthusiasts.

Palamós has a long, fine sandy beach where things are relatively quiet. You can take a wonderful walk along the promenade round the bay and beach below the town. There are some cafes and now and again there are even locals to be seen dancing the *sardana* on the promenade.

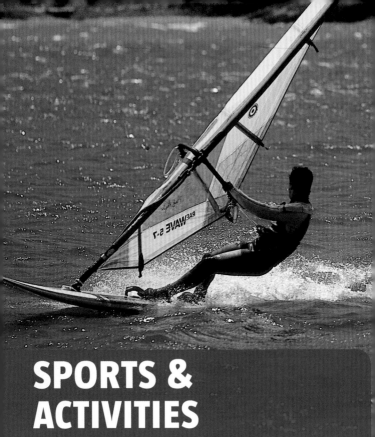

SPORTS & ACTIVITIES

Water sports enthusiasts are in heaven on the Costa Brava, its sheltered bays and ports, are ideal for sailors, windsurfers and divers.

The unspoilt flora and fauna of the nature reserves, such as Illes Medes, make for particularly exciting dive destinations. But the Costa Brava also offers golfers and hikers plenty of opportunities. And if you want to play tennis, you will not need to look around for long, as all the better hotels have their own court.

BALLOON TRIPS

You can book this adventure with Globus Empordà who provide flights over Baix Empordà and Alt Empordà. The altitude of balloon depends on the weather. The trip lasts up to 90 minutes and costs 160 euros for adults, 100 euros for children up to 14 years. There is an impressive 2-minute video on their website to whet your appetite. *Tel. 6 20 84 67 42 | www.globus emporda.com*

BEACH VOLLEYBALL

Beach volleyball is very popular throughout the Costa Brava in the summer. Often it is just a case of some visitors to the beach spontaneously starting up a game,

Photo: Windsurfers at Port de la Selva

Tee off, serve, ride the waves: there are just as many golf courses and tennis courts as good windsurfing, sailing and diving

but sometimes local businesses sponsor volleyball tournaments, with the winners receiving small prizes. On most beaches the nets are left set up for the whole summer. And, as a rule, joining in is free.

DIVING

The rocky coastline with lots of bays only accessible from the sea is a popular diving area. The water is relatively clear and calm, especially in summer. Most dive centres close in the winter.

The nature reserve islands *Illes Medes* off L'Estartit, are highly rated by divers and snorkelers by virtue of their varied marine life. Scuba diving is only permitted in certain sections of the coastal area of the Parc Natural del Cap de Creus. You can obtain information from *Reserva Marina,*

This is what makes hiking fun: fantastic views of the coast at Calella de Palafrugell

the office for island protection, and from tourist offices.

GOLF

The landscape of gentle hills provides the ideal conditions for golfers. Wetlands and winter rainfall ensure that the greens and fairways are always lush and green. You can obtain comprehensive information including course maps at *www.golfincosta brava.org* which provides links to all the local courses at Girona, Pals, Peralada, Platja d'Aro and Lloret de Mar. Green fees for a round on these 18-hole courses normally start at 50 euros.

HIKING

The Costa Brava, the hinterland and the south-east section of the Pyrenees offer hiking opportunities at all ability levels. Two international hiking trails cross the country. The INSIDER TIP GR 11 begins in

the Parc Natural del Cap de Creus reserve and ends on the other side of the peninsula on the Atlantic. The GR 92 follows the coast in a north/south direction. Information on less demanding hikes is available from the local tourist offices. You can obtain general information and tips at the *Centre Excursionista de Catalunya (Carrer Paradis, 10 | Barcelona | tel. 9 33 15 23 11)*. At the main office of the *Parc Natural del Cap de Creus (Sant Pere de Rodes | tel. 9 72 19 31 91 | www.parcsdecatalunya.net)* there is lots of information and especially INSIDER TIP outstanding maps about the hiking trails in the park.

HORSE RIDING

Horse rides and riding lessons for beginners are provided by *Hípica Aiguamolls* for 25 euros per hour. *Hípica Aiguamolls | Ctr. de Palau de Saverdera à Castelló | Empúries | tel. 9 72 45 05 45 | info@ haguamolls.com*

KAYAKING

It is mainly sea kayaking which is available. At the *Estació Nàutica* in L'Estartit *(tel. 9 72 75 06 99 | www.enestartit.com)* you can book a five-hour kayak course from 70 euros. The company has bases in Llançà, Cadaqués and Roses. *SK-Kayak Llança (Carrer Farella, 25 | tel. 6 27 43 33 32 | www.skkayak.com)* offers trial courses for sea kayaking *(3 hrs from 50 euros)* and also rents out kayaks.

MOUNTAIN BIKING

In Spanish mountain biking is called *bicicleta todo terreno*, in short BTT. Some communities have *Centros BTT* which are used as the meeting place for mountain bikers and the starting point for various tours. You can also get help with repairs, bikes can be hired, and showers are also available. The *Centre BTT in Baix Empordà (Av. del Carrilet, s/n | Castell d'Aro | tel. 9 72 82 51 51)* is based in the old railway station in Castell d'Aro. You will find information about various routes in the area at the website *www.costabravacentre.org/en/index.htm.* In Girona there are some bike shops and also a BTT base: *Centre BTT El Gironès | Carrer del Tren, s/n | tel. 9 72 46 82 42 | btt@girones.cat.*

SAILING

Almost every coastal resort has a marina and a sailing club. Local sailors are members of the *Clubs Nàutics* which – usually along with lots of restaurants – are situated right on the port and also allow guests. Here you can enquire about everything to do with boat hire, local providers and weather and sea conditions. The *Club Nàutic L'Escala (L'Escala | tel. 9 72 77 00 16 | www.nauticescala.com)* provides a twelve-hour basic dinghy sailing course from 175

euros. At *Costa Màgica (tel. 9 72 32 33 07)* in St Feliu de Guíxols you can book an eight-hour sailing trip including swim, snorkel and drink from 80 euros. General information about diving is available at the *Association of Sub Aqua Centres (Carrer Closa del Llop, 109 | Apartado, 178 | L'Escala | tel. 9 72 77 00 66).* This association represents 33 diving centres. At Tossa de Mar you can book diving courses for all levels of ability under expert supervision at the water sports centre *Cala Llevadó (tel. 9 72 34 18 66 | www.cll-watersports.com).* You can also hire equipment and diving boats.

TENNIS

Tennis does not seem to be particularly popular with tourists. As a rule the major hotels have their own tennis court, use of which is included in the price for accommodation. There is a tennis club with 14 courts, pool and restaurant in Platja d'Aro *(Club de Tennis Platja d'Aro | 9am–10pm | Paratge la Gramoia | tel. 9 72 81 74 00).* You can find a link to clubs in the area at *costabrava.angloinfo.com*

WINDSURFING

The bay at El Port de la Selva is especially popular with local windsurfers. There are wide surfing areas in the Bay of Roses and Bay of Pals. Sant Pere de Pescador, in the Bay of Roses, is the venue for the PWA windsurfing world championships.
From March to the middle of November, the windsurfing school *Llançà Escola Windsurf (tel. 9 72 38 13 88 | www.windiscovery.com)* provides beginner lessons from 45 euros. This company also runs four windsurfing centres in Roses *(Platja de Roses, at the tourist information)* and in Port de la Selva, C/Llançà. *Main office: Llança, Av. Mestra, 34 | tel. 9 72 38 13 88 | www.windiscovery.com*

TRAVEL WITH KIDS

Catalans are in general child-friendly people and so small children and young guests are welcomed on the Costa Brava.

Parents need to bear in mind that their children can easily get lost in the hubbub of the tourist centres or in Barcelona's big city hustle and bustle. It is important, therefore, that even youngest children know precisely where they are staying. On the Costa Brava, especially in the seaside resorts, there is varied (and usually free) children's entertainment throughout the summer.

In addition to sports events, the communities organise engaging and creative concerts, magic shows, theatrical productions, fire work displays and crafts activities. The local tourist offices publish programmes and timetables of what is on, where and when.

ALT EMPORDÀ

AQUABRAVA WATER PARK
(121 D5) (*ⅡⅡ G5*)
Enormous slides, rapids, swimming pools and restaurants – a paradise for children. *June–mid Sept daily 10am–7pm | admission 25 euros, children up to 1.20m 15 euros | Roses | Carretera Cadaqués Les Garrigues | www.aquabrava.com*

Photo: Underwater tunnel in the aquarium in Barcelona

Cool tips (not only) for water lovers: water parks with huge slides are fun for everyone, and there is no chance of getting bored

BUTTERFLY PARK
(121 D5) (𝄢 F5)

The massive greenhouse recreates a tropical rainforest and is full of colourful and rare butterflies in natural surroundings. *Feb–Oct Mon–Fri 9am–midday and 3pm–6pm, Sat 10am–1pm | admission 5 euros, children up to 14 years 3 euros | Empúria-brava | road to Castelló, approx. 8km/5mi | www.butterflypark.es/eng/node/55*

AQUADIVER WATER WORLD
(125 E3) (𝄢 F11)

This large water park offers lots of fun for children of all ages — there are several swimming pools and long water slides. *June–Nov daily 10am–6.30pm | admission 26.50 euros, children up to 1.40m 15 euros, children up to 1m free | Carretera de*

Circumvallació, s/n | Platja d'Aro | www. aquadiver.com

INSIDER TIP **CLUB INFANTIL**
(121 D5) (*Ⓜ G5*)

In summer the town council in Roses offers children (3–10 years) a varied leisure programme with trained supervisors. *Platja Nova, opposite the tourist office | Roses*

MUSEU D'HISTÒRIA DE LA JOGUINA
(125 E3–4) (*Ⓜ E–F11*)

This museum has more than 2500 historic toys on display – all in perfect working order. *15 June–12 Sept daily 5pm–9pm, 13 Sept–14 June Tue–Fri 10am–1pm and 4pm–7pm, Sat 10am–1pm and 4pm–8pm, Sun 11am–2pm | admission 4 euros, children under 8 years free | Rambla Vidal, 48–50 | Sant Feliu de Guíxols | tel. 9 72 82 22 49 | www.museudelajoguina.cat*

PIRATE SAILING SHIP
(123 F3) (*Ⓜ G7*)

El Corsari Negre, the Black Corsar, is a wooden sailing ship which is modelled on a pirate ship. It sails from L'Estartit along the coast, one route heading north to Sant Martí d'Empúries, the other south to Cap de Begur. *Tours 1.5–5 hrs, booking recommended | ticket prices adults from 25 euros, children from 13 euros | C/ de la Platja, 10am–1pm and 3pm–6.30pm | L'Estartit | tel. 9 72 75 14 89 | www.nautilus. es/corsarinegre*

SNORKELING
(123 F3) (*Ⓜ G7*)

Children can learn how to snorkel under expert guidance with the outdoor activities provider Medaqua. *June–mid Sept | booking recommended | 2.5 hrs children 20 euros, from 12 years 25 euros | Passeig Marítim, 13 | L'Estartit | tel. 9 72 75 20 43 | www.medaqua.com*

DIVE TRIPS (123 F3) (*Ⓜ G7*)

A trip on the *Nautilus Illes Medes* diving boat is an adventure and makes the experience of diving more interesting than the underwater world itself. *All year | trip from 18.50 euros, children up to 11 years from 11.50 euros | Passeig Marítim, 23 | L'Estartit | tel. 9 72 75 14 89 | www. nautilus.es*

TOURÍST TRAIN THROUGH SANT FELIU DE GUÍXOLS (125 E3–4) (*Ⓜ E–F11*)

A trip on the *Carrilet Ganxó,* a bus which looks like a train, can be great fun. It takes passengers to the town's main sights. *Price 5 euros | information about times and routes in the tourist office | tel. 9 72 82 00 51*

GIRONA AND LA SELVA

INSIDER TIP **MINICLUB INFANTIL**
(124 C5) (*Ⓜ D12*)

A play centre is set up on the town beach in Lloret de Mar in summer, providing supervised activities, games and events, for children from 3–12. *June–mid Sept Mon–Fri 11am–6pm, Sat and Sun 3pm–6pm | admission free | Playa de Lloret*

VIAJES MARÍTIMOS
(124 C5) (*Ⓜ D12*)

Boots cruise along the coast from Lloret to Blanes in the south or to Palamós in the north and other ports. A trip from Lloret to Palamós, costs 19.50 euros, to Sant Feliu 16 euros. *Contact only by tel. 9 72 36 90 95 | www.viajesmaritimos.com*

WATER WORLD (124 C5) (*Ⓜ D12*)

Enormous water park with rapids, swimming pools, slides, wave pool and a water roller coaster! Only open from May to mid September. *May and mid–end Sept daily 10am–6pm, June and start–mid Sept daily 10am–6.30pm, July and Aug daily*

10am–7pm | admission from 30 euros, children up to 0.80m free, up to 1.20m 15 euros | Carretera Vidreres 1.2km | Lloret de Mar | www.waterworld.es

BARCELONA

AQUARIUM ● (U E4) (𝔐 e4)

This is one of the most interesting aquariums in Europe, with all of the most important Mediterranean plants and marine life. The main attraction is the large underwater tunnel with a close-up view of sharks and octopuses. An interactive area for a hands-on experience of the Mediterranean underwater world. *July and Aug daily 9.30am–11pm, Sept–June Mon–Fri 9.30am–9pm, Sat and Sun 9.30am–9.30pm | admission 19 euros, children (5–10 years) 14 euros, children (3–4 years) 5 euros | Moll d'Espanya (Maremagnum) | www.aquariumbcn.com*

COSMO CAIXA BARCELONA
(0) (𝔐 0)

In the science museum children learn in an entertaining way how mechanics function, how optical lenses work and how objects are perceived. In addition there is a weather station, a planetarium, workshops on how to handle animals as well as regular exhibitions. *Tue–Sun 10am–8pm | admission 4 euros, children 2 euros, on special occasions 1.50 euros supplement | Isaac Newton, 26 | FGC stop Av. del Tibidabo | www.fundacio.lacaixa.es*

RAMBLAS
(U C5–D3) (𝔐 c5–d3)

For children this offers great fun in the heart of the city as there is always plenty of activity: funny puppets playing the piano, clowns encouraging children to join in and play and all for a donation of just a few cents.

Building sand castles at the seaside: fun everywhere on the Costa Brava

FESTIVALS & EVENTS

In addition to the regular national and religious holidays, there are lots of other events on the Costa Brava, such as historic festivals (Girona) or music festivals, also with international participation (Peralada, Torroella). The dates vary from year to year so enquire in the local tourist offices.

OFFICIAL HOLIDAYS

1 Jan *New Year's Day*; **6 Jan** *Epiphany*; **Holy Week** *Good Friday*; *Easter Monday*; **1 May** *Labour Day*; **24 June** *St John's Day*; **15 Aug** *Assumption Day*; **11 Sept** *National Day of Catalonia*; **24 Sept** *Barcelona's patron saint, only here a holiday*; **12 Oct** *Columbus discovers America*; **1 Nov** *All Saints*; **6 Dec** *Constitution Day*; **8 Dec** *Immaculate Conception*; **25/26 Dec** *Christmas*

SPECIAL EVENTS

JANUARY
28: ▶ *Festa Major* in Tossa de Mar, fireworks, *sardanas* and funfair

FEBRUARY/MARCH
▶ *Carnival* in almost all the major towns and resorts, especially in Girona, with processions and street dances

MARCH/APRIL
▶ ★ *Semana Santa*, Easter Week, is marked in almost all the communities with processions

APRIL
23: ▶ INSIDER TIP ▶ *Sant Jordi*, the patron saint of Catalonia, is celebrated everywhere with processions, *sardanas* and street parties

MAY
From 3: ▶ *Festa de la Santa Creu,* the Festival of the Holy Cross, is observed in Figueres with fireworks, processions and *sardanas*
Mid May: ▶ *Temps de Flors,* flower festival in Girona, public buildings, streets and the cathedral steps are all decorated with a sea of flowers

JUNE
22–26: ▶ *Festa Major* in Palamós, the town's patron saint is honoured with fireworks, dancing and *sardanas*

Patron saints are honoured at the Festas Majores with dancing, processions and funfairs, very often including the traditional *sardanas*

23–24: ▶ INSIDERTIP *Sant Joan* (also known as Midsummer's Eve) is ushered in with dancing and fireworks

JULY/AUGUST

16: ▶ INSIDERTIP *Festa del Carme:* the patron saint of fishermen is celebrated in Cadaqués, but also in most other ports, with boat processions, dancing and street parties

23–26: ▶ *Festa Major* in Lloret de Mar and Blanes. *Sardanas,* street dancing and funfair

25: ▶ ● *Concurso de Sardanas,* traditional *sardanas* competition in Sant Feliu de Guíxols

End of July: international ▶ *Firework Competition* in Blanes. Pyrotechnicians from many countries show off their skills over four days

July/August: international ▶ *Music Festival* in Torroella de Montgrí

AUGUST

25: ▶ *Festa Major* in Toroella de Montgrí, funfair, *sardanas* and fireworks. There are similar festivities in the last week of August at the ▶ *Festa Major* in Llafranc

SEPTEMBER

11: ▶ *La Diada:* the National Day of Catalonia is celebrated in many places with processions and *sardanas*

Third Sunday: ▶ *Festa Major* in Begur

OCTOBER/NOVEMBER

23 Oct–1 Nov: ▶ *Festas de Sant Narcís:* *sardanas* and dancing as well as cultural events

DECEMBER

Pre-Christmas period: ▶ *Fira de Santa Llúcia,* Christmas market outside the cathedral in Barcelona

LINKS, BLOGS, APPS & MORE

LINKS

▶ en.costabrava.org The official website of the Costa Brava Tourist Board, everything you need to know: things to do, a route planner with interactive map, events calendar and online bookings etc.

▶ www.spain.info/en The Spanish Tourist Office website contains a wealth of information. Art lovers should search for Dalí and will find lots of interesting facts

about him as well as an overview of the places, mainly on the Costa Brava, where his works can be admired. There is also an excellent 3-minute video

▶ costabrava.angloinfo.com Though intended more for expats living here than tourists, there is still lots of up-to-date information about the region, including the latest events, news and a discussion forum

▶ nauticcostabrava.com This is a website for water sports enthusiasts. Whether snorkelling, water skiing, kayaking and lots more, you will find everything about water sports on the Costa Brava: locations, activities, maps, photos. There is a good description of all the beaches on the coast!

▶ www.barcelona-tourist-guide.com This is a comprehensive site full of tourist information with links to suggested walks round Barcelona and an interactive map showing the city's various sights

BLOGS & FORUMS

▶ lloret-de-mar-stuff.blogspot.co.uk This award winning blog has lots of insider information about Lloret de Mar: events, excursions, restaurants, pubs, bars and nightlife

▶ www.ottsworld.com/blogs Follow the links to Spain and you will come to the observations of an American journalist Sherry Ott. Check out her comments in 'Under the Catalan Sun' – opinionated but interesting

Regardless of whether you are still preparing your trip or already on the Costa Brava: these addresses will provide you with more information, videos and networks to make your holiday even more enjoyable

▶ www.youtube.com/watch?v=aFCeI 6VAoPU 'Costa Brava from the air' – it is rather fragmented and has rather obtrusive music instead of commentary, but there are some stunning images

▶ www.spain-holiday.com/Costa-Brava The site contains a very informative video giving a comprehensive tour of the region, with lots of other useful information

▶ www.cbsnews.com/video/watch/?id=50142498n A short video showing current construction work on the Sagrada Familia, giving a clear impression of the awesome structure and the huge amount of work needed to complete it

▶ www.travelchannel.com/video/catalonias-sardana-dance-11164 A video about the sardana, the Catalan national dance: how it is danced and what shoes you need!

▶ apps.barcelonaturisme.com Download an app for every occasion to your mobile device: if you are new to the city, if you are looking for a place to eat, if you are a fan of architecture or history, this is the best way to get to know Barcelona at your own pace

▶ appshopper.com/travel/ispain-2 The app is free and provides information about events, restaurants and sights in Spain, news and travel, weather forecasts and translator

▶ itunes.apple.com You can download a Costa Brava Beaches app which contains a guide to more than 70 beaches, weather forecasts, images, a virtual tour, webcams, etc.

▶ short.travel/cbr5 Tripwolf community members show their favourite places in Barcelona – churches, museums and other sights – and give restaurant and shopping tips

▶ short.travel/cbr10 You will find details about private accommodation and their owners, with reviews

TRAVEL TIPS

ARRIVAL

✈ There are numerous airlines offering cheap flights to Barcelona from various UK airports. Jet2 fly from Manchester and Leeds Bradford (www.jet2.com); easyJet fly from Liverpool, Bristol, Newcastle, Belfast and Luton (www.easyjet.com); Ryanair (www.ryanair.com) also fly from Liverpool, as well as from Cardiff, Stansted, Birmingham, Leeds Bradford, East Midlands, Shannon and Prestwick; Monarch fly from Birmingham, Manchester and East Midlands (www.monarch.com); and Flybe from Exeter and Southampton (www.flybe.com).

🚗 You can get to the Costa Brava by car from Calais in a day (800mi), though you'd be advised to break the journey. Be aware that motorway charges in France and Spain are high and, if you have time, you should use the toll-free national roads in France and the autovías in Spain. There is also an Auto Train service from Paris to Narbonne. Information: tel. 08448 484 050 | www.raileurope.co.uk

🚆 You can now travel from London to Barcelona by high-speed train in a single day from £98 one-way with a glass of wine to hand and not an airport security queue in sight. Take a morning Eurostar from St Pancras and you can have breakfast in London, lunch in Paris and your evening meal in Barcelona! Or, for a real indulgence, take an afternoon Eurostar to Paris, then the excellent overnight Elipsos trainhotel from Paris to Barcelona: the trainhotels have cosy bedrooms, a restaurant and café-bar. Information: www.seat61.com/Spain

🚌 There are coach services from the UK to Barcelona and they are quite cheap; however this is arguably not the best form of transport for such a long journey. The 24-hour trip from London to Barcelona, for example, will cost around £150 for a return ticket. Information: www.eurolines.co.uk/destinations/spain. From Estación del Norte in Barcelona there are service buses to the main towns on the Costa Brava.

RESPONSIBLE TRAVEL

It doesn't take a lot to be environmentally friendly whilst travelling. Don't just think about your carbon footprint whilst flying to and from your holiday destination but also about how you can protect nature and culture abroad. As a tourist it is especially important to respect nature, look out for local products, cycle instead of driving, save water and much more. If you would like to find out more about eco-tourism please visit: www.ecotourism.org

CAMPING

Because the landscape is ideal for camping, in Catalonia there is an above average number of campsites of all standards. Although some coastal sites have a lot more sites, you need to bear in mind that even these are quickly fully booked in summer. Arguably the best site is at Cala Llevado, where there are four beaches for the price of one on the rocky cliffs, with everything from a cosy little pirate cove to a naturist beach and a sweeping bay. You will find further information at *www.campingsingirona.com* and *www.leading-campings.co.uk/campsite-Costa-Brava*. The tourist offices will also provide you with a list of camp sites.

CAR HIRE

If you prefer the flexibly of having your own transport on the Costa Brava, then a hire car is the best option. The cheapest rates for a small car for one week are under 20 euros. You have to pay an on the spot deposit of up to 400 euros, and when you pick up the car you need a credit card and driving licence. You are also advised to study the hire conditions carefully, in particular whether the contract includes fully comprehensive insurance and/or an excess in the case of damage.

COMMUNICATION

Catalans have the reputation of being reserved towards strangers. However, those involved in the tourist industry are by nature more open and outgoing. *Català* has been the official language in Catalonia since it became autonomous in 1977, after Franco's death. But even if the locals speak Catalan amongst themselves, they can all understand and speak Spanish. So if you speak Spanish, you will have no difficulties. But the same cannot be said about English. In the tourist centres such as Lloret de Mar you will get by in restaurants and hotels when placing your order or asking questions in English, and you should be able to chat to younger people in English. But the pride of the Catalans in their own language is driving a remarkable linguistic renaissance, extending from signposts in Catalan to the websites of various tourist service providers which are not translated into either Spanish or English.

CONSULATES & EMBASSIES

BRITISH CONSULATE
Avenida Diagonal 477, 13 | 08036, Barcelona | tel. +34 9 33 66 62 00, emergency out of hours tel. +34 6 06 98 76 26

US CONSULATE
Pg Elisenda Montcada 23 | 08034, Barcelona | tel. +34 9 32 80 22 27 | Mon–Fri 9.30am–1pm | www.barcelona.usconsulate.gov

CANADIAN EMBASSY
Torre Espacio, Paseo de la Castellana 259 D | 28049 | Madrid | tel. 9 13 82 84 00

CUSTOMS

In principle there are no customs duties in the EU for items intended for private consumption. For the following amounts it is assumed the item is for private use, and duty is payable on anything in excess: 800 cigarettes, 400 cigarillos, 200 cigars, 1kg smoking tobacco, 10L of spirits, 20L of liqueur, 90L of wine (including a maximum of 60L of sparkling wine), 110L of beer. You will find more details at *www.hmrc.gov.uk/customs and www.cbp.gov/xp/cgov/travel*

DRIVING

The maximum speed limit in built-up areas is 50km/30mi, on country roads 90km/56mi and on motorways 120km/75mi per

BUDGETING

Coffee	£1.40/$2.20	*for a cup in a café*
Tapas	£2.40–£4.10/$3.90–$6.50	*for one portion*
Wine	£1.20/$2	*for a glass*
Lounger	from £5/$8	*for a day*
Petrol	£1.10/$1.70	*for 1L Super*
Taxi	£1.10/$1.70	*per kilometre*

hour. The alcohol limit is 0.5ml. British citizens who don't hold a licence conforming to the EU three-part printed pink document must have an international driving licence, and you are advised to have fully comprehensive insurance. In the case of a traffic accident, you should secure two (ideally Spanish) witnesses as soon as possible and inform your own insurance company. Do not sign any acknowledgement of responsibility! In the case of minor accidents, it is best to come to an agreement with the other party. In the case of more serious collisions (involving personal injury) you should call the police, which you can do in English on *902 102 112*. In the case of breakdown, you must wear a warning vest if you are outside the vehicle. You can find out more about driving in Spain at *www.spain.info/en_GB/antes_del_viaje/consejos-practicos/conducir_en_espana/*.

ELECTRICITY

The current is 220 volts, but British electrical items will work with the correct travel plug adaptor to convert the UK standard 3 pin to Spanish 2 pin socket. North American visitors should also bring a transformer.

EMERGENCY SERVICES

General emergency number: *tel. 112*

FARM HOLIDAYS

You can spend a holiday on a farm in Catalonia too. You will find information at the *umbrella organisation Agroturismo*: *www.agroturisme.com*

HEALTH

The European Health Insurance Card (EHIC) is valid in Spain and entitles the holder to the same treatment at the same cost as a national of that country. If you don't have one, apply for one on line at *www.dh.gov.uk/travellers* – it is free. But note that the card is only valid for state provided services and not private hospitals or treatment. For further information, see *www.costa brava.angloinfo.com/information/health care*. Visitors from North America are advised to ensure they have health insurance. There is a *hospital* in all the major towns and resorts on the Costa Brava; in the villages the *Dispensari Medic* (medical centres) are usually staffed by a doctor but, at the very least, by a qualified nurse. Ask in your hotel for information about the nearest doctor's surgery.

HOSTELS

There are five youth hostels on the Costa Brava, three of them in Barcelona. You can obtain a list with charges at *Xarxa d'Albergs de Catalunya (Carrer Calàbria, 147 | 08015 Barcelona | www.xanascat.cat)*. Reservations are made on the following number: *tel. 9 34 83 83 41*

INFORMATION

SPANISH TOURIST OFFICE
– *Sixth Floor, 64 North Row, London W1K 7DE | tel. 020 73 17 20 11 | only by appointment | www.spain.info/en_GB*
– *60 East 42nd Street, Suite 5300 (5th floor), New York NY 10165-0039 | nuevayork@ tourspain.es | www.spain.info/en_US*
– *2 Bloor Street West, 34th floor, Toronto | tel. 416 961 3131 | oronto@tourspain.es*

INTERNET CAFÉS & WI-FI

Wi-Fi is now widely available in many hotels, cafés and in official buildings. Wi-Fi is provided in Spain by the Wireless Ethernet Compatibility Alliance. Almost every tourist resort on the Costa Brava has an Internet café. And public libraries also usually have Internet access.

MONEY & CREDIT CARDS

As a rule banks are open Mon–Fri 9am–1.30pm. You can withdraw cash from ATMs (charge of approx. 5 euros) with the usual cards. The *cajas*, comparable to savings banks, charge lower fees than the major banks. Lots of restaurants, hotels and shops accept the usual credit cards (Visa being most frequently used).

NEWSPAPERS

You can get, often on the day of publication, newspapers and magazines from all the EU countries in all the major towns and resorts on the Costa Brava. Regional newspapers are in Spanish and *Català*.

OPENING HOURS

As a rule the shops in the tourist resorts are open longer than in the towns inland. There are different opening hours for the

CURRENCY CONVERTER

£	€	€	£
1	1.20	1	0.85
3	3.60	3	2.55
5	6	5	4.25
13	15.60	13	11
40	48	40	34
75	90	75	64
120	144	120	100
250	300	250	210
500	600	500	425

$	€	€	$
1	0.75	1	1.30
3	2.30	3	3.90
5	3.80	5	6.50
13	10	13	17
40	30	40	50
75	55	75	97
120	90	120	155
250	185	250	325
500	370	500	650

For current exchange rates see www.xe.com

winter and the summer season (April–September) at the coastal resorts. Even state shops, such as the post office, have different opening hours from place to place. But you will not go far wrong if you keep to the following basic times: shops are open as a rule from 9am–1.30pm and from 5pm–8pm. Tourist offices are open from approx. 10am –1pm, and then again from 5pm–8pm.

PERSONAL SAFETY

Costa Brava is basically a safe holiday area. But here, as elsewhere, the old adage applies: an open door may tempt a saint. You should never leave your belongings unattended in a restaurant or bus station, and this applies particularly to Barcelona. Wherever tourists are to be found in significant numbers, thieves will not be far away. Bag and purse snatching is very common in the narrow streets of Barrio Gotic and Barrio Chino. If you are sitting outside on the terrace in a restaurant on the Ramblas, on no account should you leave a camera, mobile phone or any other valuables on the table – roaming thieves make off with such items very quickly and can easily disappear in the crowd.

PHONE & MOBILE PHONE

The international dialling code for Spain is *0034* (there is no longer a dialling code within Spain), for the UK *0044* and for the US and Canada *001*. You then dial the area code without *0* then the number. *Telephone information*: national *118 18*, international *118 25*

Public phone boxes are gradually being converted to card phones. Phone cards *(tarjeta telefónica)* can be obtained from many tobacconists, kiosks and post offices for about 6–12 euros.

A mobile phone is called a *móvil* in Spanish. Telefónica is still the dominant provider for incoming calls on non-Spanish mobile phones. You can save roaming charges by choosing the network with the lowest rates. If you have a Spanish prepaid card there are no charges for incoming calls, and the best prepaid card providers are Happy Movil, Lebara, Simya and Yoigo. You will find prices and deals at *www. memobilerental.com*. To avoid any expensive surprises, you should also make sure that you switch off all automatic services (for example software updates etc.) for the duration of your stay. North American visitors need to be aware that Spanish GSM technology is not compatible with that in Canada and the US.

POST

Opening hours as a rule: Mon–Fri 9am–1pm and 4pm–6pm, Sat 9am–1pm. The post office *(Correos y Telégrafos)* limit their activities to purely postal services. You can not phone from here, but occasionally you may be able to send emails or faxes. However, the relevant private services are better value for money. Within Europe standard letters up to 20 g and postcards cost 70 cents, overseas 78 cents. You can also buy stamps at tobacconists.

PRICES

Spanish products such as wine and brandy are cheaper than in the UK. There are lots of common prescription-free medicines, such as aspirin, which cost less than at home.

PUBLIC TRANSPORT

If you want to travel round the Costa Brava by bus, you have the choice between various bus companies, such as SARFA and AUTOCARES PUJOL, which provide a very regular service to the main towns and resorts on the coast. These companies also provide a direct service between Barcelona Airport and the Costa Brava. The Spanish State Railways RENFE provide an almost hourly service between Barcelona and the French border, calling at Girona, Figueres and Portbou. *www.sarfa.com, www.trans pujol.com, www.renfe.es*

SMOKING

Prohibido fumar, 'No smoking', is the notice you will see all over Spain since January 2011. And the anti-smoking laws have since been tightened and smoking is now banned in restaurants, bars, pubs and discos, and also in public buildings such as airports, and not even smoking areas are permitted in the workplace nor in pubs and restaurants.

TAXI

In all the major towns and resorts there are taxi stands at the markets, bus stations or in the vicinity of the main shopping streets. Make sure that the driver switches on the meter. If not, then immediately agree on the price before you set off.

TIPPING

If the service is good, it is customary to add a tip 5 to 10 per cent depending on

the amount. Tour guides also expect to be tipped.

WEATHER & WHEN TO GO

The Costa Brava enjoys a predominantly mild climate, though in recent years the heat here in high summer has occasionally become almost unbearable. Whilst the sea wind can be pleasantly cooling during the day, it can become quite cool at the coast after nightfall. The best time to travel is between Easter and early October. In summer you should, if possible, not plan your trip for August because that is the main holiday period in Spain – with all the accompanying hordes of holidaymakers.

WEATHER IN BARCELONA

	Jan	Feb	March	April	May	June	July	Aug	Sept	Oct	Nov	Dec
Daytime temperatures in °C/°F	13/55	14/57	16/61	18/64	22/72	25/77	27/81	28/82	26/79	22/72	17/63	14/57
Nighttime temperatures in °C/°F	6/43	7/45	8/46	11/52	14/57	17/63	21/70	21/70	18/64	14/57	10/50	7/45
Sunshine hours/day	5	6	6	8	8	9	10	9	7	5	5	4
Precipitation days/month	4	5	5	6	6	4	3	4	6	7	6	5
Water temperatures in °C/°F	13/55	12/54	13/55	14/57	16/61	19/66	22/72	24/75	22/72	20/67	16/61	14/57

USEFUL PHRASES CATALAN

PRONUNCIATION

c	like "s" before "e" and "i" (e.g. Barcelona);
	like "k" before "a", "o" and "u" (e.q. Casa)
ç	pronounced like "s" (e.g. França)
g	like "s" in "pleasure" before "e" and "i"; like "g" in "get" before "a", "o" and "u"
l·l	pronounced like "l"
que/qui	the "u" is always silent, so "qu" sounds like "k" (e.g. perquè)
v	at the start of a word and after consonants like "b" (e.g. València)
x	like "sh" (e.g. Xina)

IN BRIEF

Yes/No/Maybe	Sí/No/Potser
Please/Thank you/Sorry	Sisplau/Gràcies/ Perdoni
May I ...?	Puc ...?
Pardon?	Com diu *(Sie)*?/Com dius *(Du)*?
I would like to .../	Voldria .../
Have you got ...?	Té ...?
How much is ...?	Quant val ...?
I (don't) like this	(no) m'agrada
good	bo/bé *(Adverb)*
bad	dolent/malament *(Adverb)*
Help!/Attention!/Caution!	Ajuda!/Compte!/Cura!
ambulance	ambulància
police/fire brigade	policia/bombers
Prohibition/forbidden	prohibició/prohibit
danger/dangerous	perill/perillós
May I take a photo here/of you?	Puc fer-li una foto aquí?

GREETINGS, FAREWELL

Good morning!/afternoon!	Bon dia!
Good evening!/night!	Bona tarda!/Bona nit!
Hello!/Goodbye!	Hola!/Adéu! Passi-ho bé!
See you	Adéu!
My name is ...	Em dic ...
What's your name?	Com es diu?

Parles Català?

"Do you speak Catalan?" This guide will help you to say the basic words and phrases in Catalan

DATE & TIME

Monday/Tuesday	dilluns/dimarts
Wednesday/Thursday	dimecres/dijous
Friday/Saturday	divendres/dissabte
Sunday/working day	diumenge/dia laborable
holiday	dia festiu
today/tomorrow/	avui/demà/
yesterday	ahir
hour/minute	hora/minut
day/night/week	dia/nit/setmana

TRAVEL

open/closed	obert/tancat
entrance/driveway	entrada
exit/exit	sortida
departure/	sortida/
departure/arrival	sortida d'avió/arribada
toilets/restrooms /	Lavabos/
ladies/gentlemen	Dones/Homes
Where is ...?/	On està ...?/
Where are ...?	On estan ...?
left/right	a l'esquerra/a la dreta
close/far	a prop/lluny
bus	bus
taxi/cab	taxi
bus stop/	parada/
cab stand	parada de taxis
parking lot/	aparcament/
parking garage	garatge
street map/map	pla de la ciutat/mapa
train station/harbour	estació/port
airport	aeroport
schedule/ticket	horario/bitllet
train / platform/track	tren/via
platform	andana
I would like to rent ...	Voldria llogar ...
a car/a bicycle	un cotxe/una bicicleta
petrol/gas station	gasolinera
petrol/gas / diesel	gasolina/gasoil
breakdown/repair shop	avaria/taller

FOOD & DRINK

Could you please book a table for tonight for four?	Voldriem reservar una taula per a quatre persones per avui al vespre
on the terrace	a la terrassa
The menu, please	la carta, sisplau
Could I please have ...?	Podria portar-me ...?
bottle/carafe/glass	ampolla/garrafa/got
salt/pepper/sugar	sal/pebrot/sucre
vinegar/oil	vinagre/oli
vegetarian/	vegetarià/vegetariana/
allergy	allèrgia
May I have the bill, please?	El compte, sisplau

SHOPPING

Where can I find...?	On hi ha ...?
I'd like .../	voldria/
I'm looking for ...	estic buscant ...
pharmacy/chemist	farmacia/drogueria
baker/market	forn/mercat
shopping center	centre comercial/gran magatzem
supermarket	supermercat
kiosk	quiosc
expensive/cheap/price	car/barat/preu
organically grown	de cultiu ecològic

ACCOMMODATION

I have booked a room	He reservat una habitació
Do you have any ... left?	Encara té ...
single room	una habitació individual
double room	una habitació doble
breakfast/half board	esmorzar/mitja pensió
full board	pensió completa
at the front/seafront	exterior/amb vistes al mar
shower/sit down bath	dutxa/bany
balcony/terrace	balcó/terrassa

BANKS, MONEY & CREDIT CARDS

bank/ATM	banc/caixer automàtic
pin code	codi secret
cash/	al comptat/
credit card	amb targeta de crèdit
change	canvi

HEALTH

doctor/dentist/paediatrician	metge/dentista/pediatre
hospital/emergency clinic	hospital/urgència
fever/pain	febre/dolor
inflamed/injured	inflamat/ferit
plaster/bandage	tireta/embenat
ointment/cream	pomada/crema
pain reliever/tablet	analgèsic/pastilla

POST, TELECOMMUNICATIONS & MEDIA

stamp/letter/postcard	segell/carta/ postal
I need a landline phone card	Necessito una targeta telefònica per la xarxa fixa
I'm looking for a prepaid card for my mobile	Estic buscant una targeta de prepagament pel mòbil
Where can I find internet access?	On em puc connectar a Internet?
Do I need a special area code?	He de marcar algun prefix determinat?
socket/adapter/charger	endoll/adaptador/carregador
computer/battery/ rechargeable battery	ordinador/bateria/ acumulador
at sign (@)	arrova
internet address	adreça d'internet (URL)
e-mail address	adreça de correu electrònic
e-mail/file/print	correu electrònic/fitxer/imprimir

LEISURE, SPORTS & BEACH

beach	platja
sunshade/lounger	para-sol/gandula

NUMBERS

0 zero	12 dotze	60 seixanta
1 un/una	13 tretze	70 setanta
2 dos/dues	14 catorze	80 vuitanta
3 tres	15 quinze	90 noranta
4 quatre	16 setze	100 cent
5 cinc	17 disset	200 dos-cents/dues-centes
6 sis	18 divuit	1000 mil
7 set	19 dinou	2000 dos mil
8 vuit	20 vint	10000 deu mil
9 nou	30 trenta	
10 deu	40 quaranta	½ mig
11 onze	50 cinquanta	¼ un quart

NOTES

MARCO POLO TRAVEL GUIDES

ALGARVE
AMSTERDAM
ANDALUCÍA
ATHENS
AUSTRALIA
AUSTRIA
BALI
  LOMBOK,
  GILI ISLANDS
BANGKOK
BARCELONA
BERLIN
BRAZIL
BRUGES, GHENT &
  ANTWERP
BRUSSELS
BUDAPEST
BULGARIA
CALIFORNIA
CAMBODIA
CANADA EAST
CANADA WEST
  ROCKIES
CAPE TOWN
  WINE LANDS,
  GARDEN ROUTE
CAPE VERDE
CHANNEL ISLANDS
CHICAGO
  & THE LAKES
CHINA
COLOGNE
COPENHAGEN
CORFU
COSTA BLANCA
  VALENCIA
COSTA BRAVA
  BARCELONA
COSTA DEL SOL
  GRANADA
CRETE
CUBA
CYPRUS
  NORTH AND
  SOUTH
DRESDEN
DUBAI
DUBLIN
DUBROVNIK &
  DALMATIAN COAST

EDINBURGH
EGYPT
EGYPT'S RED
  SEA RESORTS
FINLAND
FLORENCE
FLORIDA
FRENCH ATLANTIC
  COAST
FRENCH RIVIERA
  NICE, CANNES &
  MONACO
FUERTEVENTURA
GRAN CANARIA
GREECE
HAMBURG
HONG KONG
  MACAU
ICELAND
INDIA
INDIA SOUTH
  GOA & KERALA
IRELAND
ISRAEL
ISTANBUL
ITALY
JORDAN
KOS
KRAKOW
LAKE GARDA

LANZAROTE
LAS VEGAS
LISBON
LONDON
LOS ANGELES
MADEIRA
  PORTO SANTO
MADRID
MALLORCA
MALTA
  GOZO
MAURITIUS
MENORCA
MILAN
MONTENEGRO
MOROCCO
MUNICH
NAPLES &
  THE AMALFI COAST
NEW YORK
NEW ZEALAND
NORWAY
OSLO
PARIS
PHUKET
PORTUGAL
PRAGUE

RHODES
ROME
SAN FRANCISCO
SARDINIA
SCOTLAND
SEYCHELLES
SHANGHAI
SICILY
SINGAPORE
SOUTH AFRICA
SRI LANKA
STOCKHOLM
SWITZERLAND
TENERIFE
THAILAND
TURKEY
TURKEY
  SOUTH COAST
TUSCANY
UNITED ARAB
  EMIRATES
USA SOUTHWEST
VENICE
VIENNA
VIETNAM
ZÁKYNTHOS

- PACKED WITH INSIDER TIPS
- BEST WALKS AND TOURS
- FULL-COLOUR PULL-OUT MAP
  AND STREET ATLAS

ROAD ATLAS

The green line   indicates the Trips & Tours (p. 88–93)
The blue line   indicates The perfect route (p. 30–31)

All tours are also marked on the pull-out map

Photo: El Port de la Selva

Exploring the Costa Brava

The map on the back cover shows how the area has been sub-divided

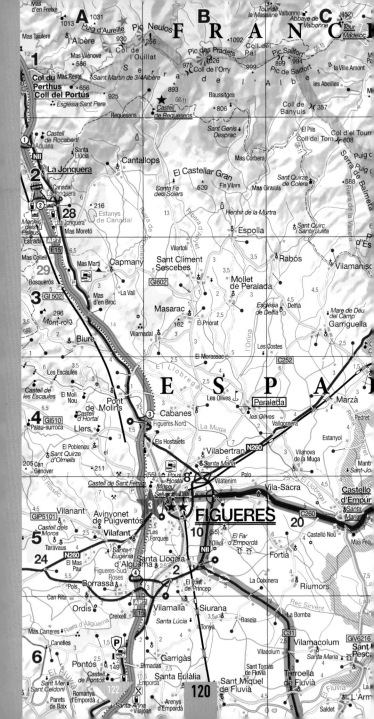

Cap Oullestrell

D **E** **F**

125 Cap
Castell

Banyuls-sur-Mer

Relg

43

la Rhetone

Cap l'Abeille

Puig
d'el Mas
180

Golf de
Séris

**Réserve
Naturelle
Marine**

Côte Vermeille

Cap Rederis

Cap Peyrefite

D914

1

505

Anse de Terrambou

Mas de
Mingou

Cerbère

Cap Cerbère

arroi

**Coll des
Balistres**

207

Coll dels Belitres

M A R

2

Portbou

(30)

Cala de las Ratas

56

Cap Marcer

M E D I T E R R À N I A

às

N260

Port de Colera

Colera

de Molinàs

Cap Llardó

67

Garbet

Badia de Cap Ras

Grifeu

Cap Res

Hostal Grifeu

Badia Llançà

Isla Castella

El Port de Llançà

Setcases

Llançà

3

Valleta

4.5

Punta s'Arenella

Cap Gros

430

168

El Golfet

Punta dels Farallons

La Vall
de Santa Creu

**El Port
de la Selva**

la Galera

95

Puig

Illa de Portaló

Dolmen del Mas
de la Mata

Sant Pere
de Rodes

**La Selva
de Mar**

de Cala Sardina

Sant Baldiri

Illa de Cullaró

S'Encalladora

A

Castell de
Sant Salvador

Parc Natural

Puig Alt Gran

82

**Cap de
Creus**

Pau

El Mas Isaac

Serra de Rodes

2.5

2

243

u-saverdera

Ermita
de Sant
Onofre

Perafita

Cala Bona

Punta d'en Codera

El Mas Fumats

433

Portlligat

Cala Portlligat

Illa de Portlligat

3.5

El Mas
Bosca

Cadaqués

(23)

Punta de
s'Oliquera

Aqua Brava

463

El Pení

S'Arenella

La Barriga

El Mas Mates

506

2/3

Santa
Margarida

Santa Maria
La Citadella

El Mas Oliva

Sant Sebastià

Badia de Cadaqués

4

Mas
Chalet

Roses

Cap de Creus

Gruta

Cala Nans

Parc

Platja Sta
Margarida

Puig Rom

Far de
Roses

Castell de
la Poncella

Montjoi

Torre de los
Sastres

Punta de sa Figuera

Badia de Roses

Cala Jóncols

5

Empuriabrava

Platja de
Canyelles
Petites

Platja de
Canyelles Grosses

Cala Montjoi

Cala Murtra

Cap de Norfeu

Cavall Bernat

Natural

Cap Trencat

Punta Falconera

Platja
de
Can
Comes

Aiguamolls

G o l f d e

de l'Empordà

R o s e s

4 km

2.49 mi

6

Platja de Sant

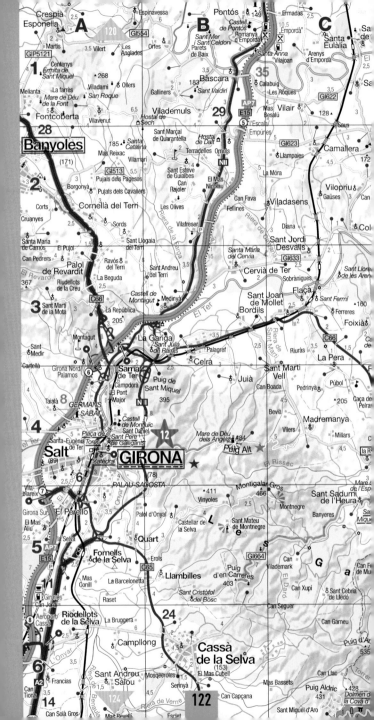

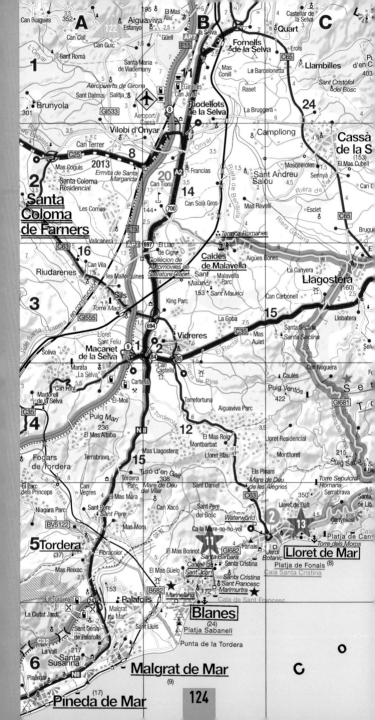

D E F

Banyeres
Sant Miquel
El Convent Fonteta
Sant Climent de Peralta
123
La Barceloneta
C66
Llofriu
S
Can Viladernark
Can Font de Mantanya
Sant Pol
Can Rauric
GR-92
Palafrugell 1
Puig Gros 305
Morena
Can Xupí
G
Sant Cebrià de Lledó
Santa Llúcia
Dolmen del Llobinar
Mont-ras
Can Seguer
GI660
Coll de la Ganga
2.5
Santa Coloma de Fitor
El Mas Flaquet
C31
Can Garneu
Puig d'Arques 535
Sant Cebrià dels Alls
Puig Cargol 362
Vall-llobrega
2
Mas Bassets
Can Llac
Torrent d'en Simona
Mas Blanquet
Sant Nazari
Calonge (37)
Mas Juni
Sant Joan de Palamós
La Fosca
Puig Aldric 431
428
Dolmen de la Cova d'en Daina
Riufred
Sant Antoni de Calonge
3.5
Cala s' Altguer
Cap Gros
Santa Maria
Sant Miquel d'Aro
Cabanyes
3.5
El Mas Vila
Palamós
3.5
Romanyà de la Selva
414
El Mas Ros
1.5
Torre Valentina
Platja de Roig (14)
2
Penedes
Bell-lloc
Sant Ampèlit
3.5
30'
C31
El Mas Vila
3
Ridaura
Santa Maria de Solius
la Roca de Malvet
Les Teules
El MasNou
La Grota
Aquadiver
Hotel Sant Jordi
Can Tallades
Solius
Sta. Cristina d'Aro
Castell d'Aro
Platja d'Aro
Platja d'Aro
Montclar 417
El Vilar
Torre Sant Josep
El Romà
5.5
6.5
Punta Prima
Puig de Cols
Mas Trempat
C65
Bufaganyes
Cala de sa Conca
Pedralta
9
s'Agaro ★★
Platja Sant Pol
Sant Amanç
Sant Baldiri
GR-92
417
Menhir del Terma Gros
2
GI682
Sant Elm
Sant Telm
Sant Pol
SANT FELIU DE GUIXOLS
Sant Grau
Canyet
Punta Brava
S Estufador de Garbí (4)
Cadiretes 518
10
Platja de Canyet
Punta del Romeguer
Cala de Salionç
Salionç
4
14
Cap Pentiner
Cala de Giverola
Cala Pola
Cala Bona
Tossa de Mar ★★
Vila Vella (60)
Cap de Tossa de sa Boquera de Llorell
B
r
5
a
t
M A R
M E D I T E R R À N I A
6

4 km
2.49 mi

Girona
Gerona

Parc Municipal de la Devesa

Passeig de la Devesa

Carrer Figuerola

Carrer Bonastruc de Porta

Passeig Canalejas

Riu Onyar

Pl. S. Feliu
Sant Feliu
Banys Arabs
Plaça Jurats
Casa Pastors
Museu d'Història
Catedral
Museu d'Art

Plaça St. Pere
Sant Nicolau
Sant Pere de Galligants
Galligants

Plaça Indepèndencia

C. Anselm Clave
Pl. Jordi de St. Jordi
Jaume 1 er
C. Hortes
Cristofel Grober
Clara
Santa
Obra
Museu del Cinema
Plaça Josep Pla
Via Avd. Sant Francesc
Carrer
Nou
Riu Onyar
Rbla. de la Llibertat

C. Ballesteries
C. de la Força
C. Alemanys
Plaça St. Domènec
Palau Agullana
Sant Domènec Universitat
Passeig fora Muralla

Carrer
de
Plaça Marques de Camps

Carrer Ciutadans
Pl. St. Josep
Sant Josep
Carrer St. Josep
Nou

Pont de Pedra
Plaça Catalunya
Ajun-tament
Teatre Municipal
Portal

Plaça Hospital
Plaça Pompeu Fabra
C. Albareda
Carrer

Gran
Ronda S. Antoni
Carrer de Joan
Carrer Bisbe Lorenzana
Pl. Sibil·la de Fortià
P. G.al Mendoza
Plaça G.al Marvà
Centre Cultural la Mercè
Jardines de la Muralla
Passeig fora Muralla

Maragall
Mercat
P. Sant Francesc
C. Ultónia
Carrer Carme
Carrer del Sol

100 m
109 yd

Figueres

Ronda Cardenal Gomà
Verdaguer
C. Cap de Creus
Carrer Canigó
Carrer de la Jonquera
B. Indústria
B. Mercer
Carrer Muralla
Carrer Peralada
C. Eres de la Vila
Carrer Rentac

Ronda
Carrer Llers
Torre Galatea
Museu Dalí
Pl. Gala i S. Dalí
C. St. Domènec
C. Pilar
C. Tins
C. Primflat
Carrer Ample
C. Sol d'Isern
C. St. Josep Sol d'Isern
C. Sant Rafael
C. Sta. Llúcia
Plaça l'Escorxad
Plaça de la Palmera

Parc Bosc Municipal
Pujada del Castell
Mossèn Cinto
C. Pep Ventura
Policia
C. Sant Pere
Plaça Pius XII
Plaça de l'Ajuntament
Ajuntament
Biblioteques
C. St. Cristófol

C. Narcís Gay
C. Àlvarez de Castro
Galligans
C. Tortellà
Carrer
Lasauca
Museu de Joguets
C. Portella
C. Joan Maragall
Girona
Museu de l'Empordà
Carrer Moreria
Carrer Monturiol
Carrer Caamaño
Carrer Blanc
Carrer Rutlla
Plaça de Catalunya

Plaça del Sol
Policia Municipal
Ronda Firal
Carrer Rodes
Carrer Villafant
Carrer Olot
Carrer Rosa
C. Príncep
C. Sant Vicenç
Carrer Sant Josep
Rambla
C. Forn Nou
Plaça Josep Pla
Teatre
Carrer Sant Pau
Jardins Josep Puig Pujades
Plaça Ernest Vila
Carrer Castel

100 m
109 yd

KEY TO ROAD ATLAS

English		Deutsch
Motorway · Toll junction · Toll station · Junction with number · Motel · Restaurant · Snackbar · Filling-station · Parking place with and without WC	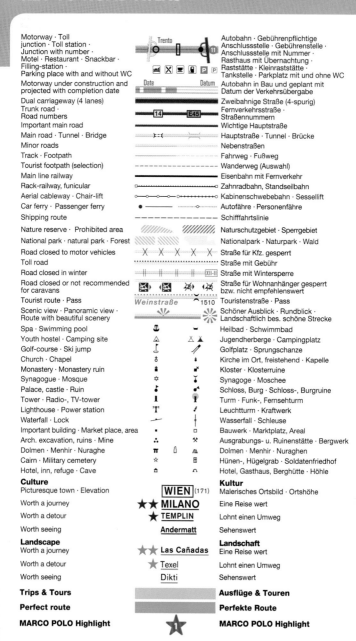	Autobahn · Gebührenpflichtige Anschlussstelle · Gebührenstelle · Anschlussstelle mit Nummer · Rasthaus mit Übernachtung · Raststätte · Kleinraststätte · Tankstelle · Parkplatz mit und ohne WC
Motorway under construction and projected with completion date		Autobahn in Bau und geplant mit Datum der Verkehrsübergabe
Dual carriageway (4 lanes)		Zweibahnige Straße (4-spurig)
Trunk road ·		Fernverkehrsstraße ·
Road numbers		Straßennummern
Important main road		Wichtige Hauptstraße
Main road · Tunnel · Bridge		Hauptstraße · Tunnel · Brücke
Minor roads		Nebenstraßen
Track · Footpath		Fahrweg · Fußweg
Tourist footpath (selection)		Wanderweg (Auswahl)
Main line railway		Eisenbahn mit Fernverkehr
Rack-railway, funicular		Zahnradbahn, Standseilbahn
Aerial cableway · Chair-lift		Kabinenschwebebahn · Sessellift
Car ferry · Passenger ferry		Autofähre · Personenfähre
Shipping route		Schifffahrtslinie
Nature reserve · Prohibited area		Naturschutzgebiet · Sperrgebiet
National park · natural park · Forest		Nationalpark · Naturpark · Wald
Road closed to motor vehicles		Straße für Kfz. gesperrt
Toll road		Straße mit Gebühr
Road closed in winter		Straße mit Wintersperre
Road closed or not recommended for caravans		Straße für Wohnanhänger gesperrt bzw. nicht empfehlenswert
Tourist route · Pass		Touristenstraße · Pass
Scenic view · Panoramic view · Route with beautiful scenery		Schöner Ausblick · Rundblick · Landschaftl. bes. schöne Strecke
Spa · Swimming pool		Heilbad · Schwimmbad
Youth hostel · Camping site		Jugendherberge · Campingplatz
Golf-course · Ski jump		Golfplatz · Sprungschanze
Church · Chapel		Kirche im Ort, freistehend · Kapelle
Monastery · Monastery ruin		Kloster · Klosterruine
Synagogue · Mosque		Synagoge · Moschee
Palace, castle · Ruin		Schloss, Burg · Schloss-, Burgruine
Tower · Radio-, TV-tower		Turm · Funk-, Fernsehturm
Lighthouse · Power station		Leuchtturm · Kraftwerk
Waterfall · Lock		Wasserfall · Schleuse
Important building · Market place, area		Bauwerk · Marktplatz, Areal
Arch. excavation, ruins · Mine		Ausgrabungs- u. Ruinenstätte · Bergwerk
Dolmen · Menhir · Nuraghe		Dolmen · Menhir · Nuraghen
Cairn · Military cemetery		Hünen-, Hügelgrab · Soldatenfriedhof
Hotel, inn, refuge · Cave		Hotel, Gasthaus, Berghütte · Höhle

Culture		**Kultur**
Picturesque town · Elevation	WIEN (171)	Malerisches Ortsbild · Ortshöhe
Worth a journey	★★ MILANO	Eine Reise wert
Worth a detour	★ TEMPLIN	Lohnt einen Umweg
Worth seeing	Andermatt	Sehenswert

Landscape		**Landschaft**
Worth a journey	★★ Las Cañadas	Eine Reise wert
Worth a detour	★ Texel	Lohnt einen Umweg
Worth seeing	Dikti	Sehenswert

Trips & Tours		**Ausflüge & Touren**
Perfect route		**Perfekte Route**
MARCO POLO Highlight	★	**MARCO POLO Highlight**

INDEX

This index lists all places, sights and beaches, plus the names of important people and key words featured in this guide. Numbers in bold indicate a main entry.

WRITE TO US

e-mail: info@marcopologuides.co.uk

Did you have a great holiday?
Is there something on your mind?
Whatever it is, let us know!
Whether you want to praise, alert us
to errors or give us a personal tip –
MARCO POLO would be pleased to
hear from you.
We do everything we can to provide the
very latest information for your trip.

Nevertheless, despite all of our authors'
thorough research, errors can creep in.
MARCO POLO does not accept any
liability for this. Please contact us by
e-mail or post.

MARCO POLO Travel Publishing Ltd
Pinewood, Chineham Business Park
Crockford Lane, Chineham
Basingstoke, Hampshire RG24 8AL
United Kingdom

PICTURE CREDITS
Cover photograph: Cadaqués, Girona province, Huber: Fantuz
Ciclus: LUIZ SIMÕES (17 top); Copa Penya Barcelonista (16 centre); DuMont Bildarchiv: Pompe (18/19), Selbach
(28, 42, 56, 64, 69), Widmann (102/103); Espaisucre – Jordi Butrón & Xano Saguer: Lola (16 top); © fotolia.com:
Desertdiver (16 bottom); R. Freyer (84); R. Gerth (20, 36/37, 67, 72, 93, 105); R. M. Gill (5, 8, 28/29, 55, 101);
R. M. Gill © Salvador Dalí, Fundació Cala-Salvador Dalí/VG Bild-Kunst, Bonn 2012 (front flap right); Huber: Cogoli
(2 bottom, 12/13, 50/51), Fantuz (1 top), Gräfenhain (front flap left, 30 right, 34, 45, 52, 62, 81, 118/119), Huber
(76/77), Leimer (10/11, 129), Ripani (2 centre bottom, 32/33); © istockphoto.com: Simone Becchetti (17 bottom);
G. Jung © Salvador Dalí, Fundació Cala-Salvador Dalí/VG Bild-Kunst, Bonn 2012 (39, 104 top); Laif: Gonzalez (3 top,
3 centre, 70/71, 82/83); mauritius images: age (2 top, 4), Alamy (2 centre top, 6, 9, 23, 26 right, 78, 98/99, 104
bottom); H. H. Schulz (1 bottom); T. Stankiewicz (7, 47, 75, 86, 103); M. Thomas (15); T. P. Widmann (26 left, 30 left,
40, 49, 60, 90, 94/95, 96); White Star: Gumm (3 bottom, 24/25, 29, 58, 88/89, 102), Stuart (27)

1st Edition 2014
Worldwide Distribution: Marco Polo Travel Publishing Ltd, Pinewood, Chineham Business Park,
Crockford Lane, Basingstoke, Hampshire RG24 8AL, United Kingdom. E-mail: sales@marcopolouk.com
© MAIRDUMONT GmbH & Co. KG, Ostfildern
Chief editor: Marion Zorn
Author: Horst H. Schulz; editor: Petra Klose
Programme supervision: Anita Dahlinger, Ann-Katrin Kutzner, Nikolai Michaelis
Picture editor: Gabriele Forst
What's hot: wunder media, Munich
Cartography road atlas & pull-out map: © MAIRDUMONT, Ostfildern
Design: milchhof: atelier, Berlin; Front cover, pull-out map cover, page 1: factor product munich
Translated from German by Neil Williamson; editor of the English edition: Margaret Howie, fullproof.co.za
Prepress: M. Feuerstein, Wigel
Phrase book in cooperation with Ernst Klett Sprachen GmbH, Stuttgart, Editorial by Pons Wörterbücher

DOS & DON'TS

A few things you should be aware of when on holiday

DON'T STOP ON THE MOTORWAY

On the section between the French border and Barcelona thieves operate in this way: a passing car makes a sign suggesting you have a damaged tyre. When you stop, the 'friendly' driver overtakes and also stops. Before you know it, your car is stripped. Caution is also advised in the picnic areas at motorway services and filling stations.

DON'T PLAY WITH FIRE

In the summer the Costa Brava and the interior are parched and the danger of fire is great, even close to the coast. So be very careful indeed with an open fire, do not discard cigarette ends, do not leave behind any litter (bottles and glass fragments are particularly dangerous)! In an emergency phone 112 at once.

DO DRESS APPROPRIATELY IN BARCELONA

The beaches close to Barcelona's centre mean that some people walk back to their hotel in a bikini or swimming trunks. In 2010 the city council launched a media campaign to put a stop to this, though there have been no fines as yet.

DO KEEP AN EYE ON YOUR VALUABLES

It is amazing how often people in cafés put cameras, mobile phones and other items of value on their table – an invitation for nimble thieves. You should also avoid hanging your bag over the back of your chair. The popular pickpocket areas are the Metro and Las Ramblas.

DON'T SPEED

Spain punishes traffic offences with some of the harshest fines in Europe. If you drive at more than 200km/125mi per hour on the motorway or at more than 110km/70mi in built-up areas, you face not only a heavy fine, but also a prison sentence of three to six months. The same applies to motorists who drink and drive and are found with more than 1.2ml blood alcohol level. Illegal parking is also severely punished.

DO BE WARY OF FLAMENCO SHOWS

Andalusia is the home of the flamenco. Huge advertisements for flamenco performances in Catalonia's holiday resorts are, therefore, to be regarded with a bit of scepticism. Often it is not worth the admission price because the shows contain nothing authentic. In Barcelona, however, there are occasionally artistically worthwhile performances by well-known flamenco interpreters.